In praise of *Recipe for a Kinder Life* ...

'*Recipe for a Kinder Life* is like getting a big hug from your nanna.
It's wholesome, comforting and nourishing. Our yearning to
rekindle a deeper connection with the land and each other is
stronger now than ever. Where to start the journey lies within
these pages.'

—Indira Naidoo

'The anti-celebrity chef Annie Smithers brings a cook's palate, a
grower's heart and a poet's soul to bear in the moving, practical,
inspiring story of her life. It's the how-to (and how-to-not!)
book I wish I'd read before starting my own kitchen garden,
complete with hothouse tips, philosophy and all the recipes you
may ever need.'

—Matthew Evans

'This is a deeply honest and personal story of a love of the
land and food. Annie takes us, warts and all, on her sustainable
journey of cultivation and cooking. Her respect for the land is
evident by the barrowload.'

—Paul Bangay OAM

Recipe for a Kinder Life

Annie Smithers

First published in Australia in 2021
by Thames & Hudson Australia Pty Ltd
11 Central Boulevard, Portside Business Park
Port Melbourne, Victoria 3207
ABN: 72 004 751 964

thamesandhudson.com.au

Some recipes in this book were originally published in *The Saturday Paper*.

24 23   5 4

Thames & Hudson Australia wishes to acknowledge that Aboriginal and Torres Strait Islander
people are the first storytellers of this nation and the traditional custodians of the land on which
we live and work. We acknowledge their continuing culture and pay respect to Elders past,
present and future.

ISBN 978-1-760-76144-8 (paperback)
ISBN 978-1-760-76222-3 (ebook)

A catalogue record for this
book is available from the
National Library of Australia

pp. viii–ix: Illustration by Clare O'Flynn
p. x: Photo by Sandy Scheltema
p. 277: Photo by Rose Wilson
All other photos by Susan Thompson and Annie Smithers

Cover design, cover illustration and titling: Daniel New
Text design and typesetting: Patrick Cannon
Editing: Sarina Rowell
Printed and bound in Australia by McPherson's Printing Group

For my darling wife, Susan.
You inspire me to live a better life every day.

Contents

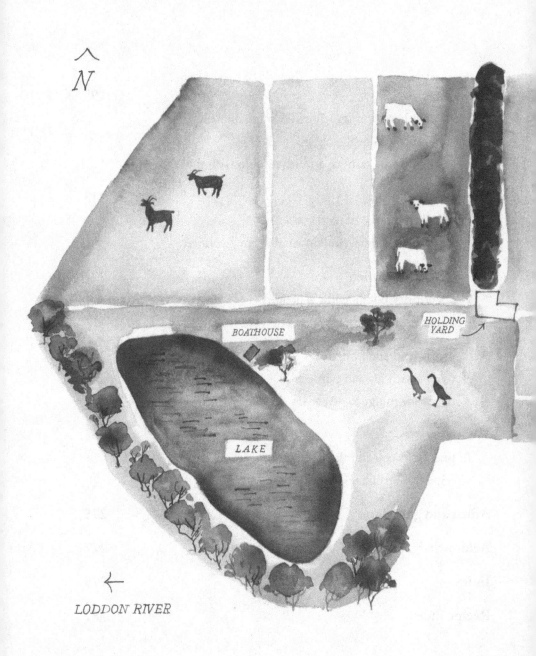

N

BOATHOUSE

HOLDING
YARD

LAKE

LODDON RIVER

Babbington Park

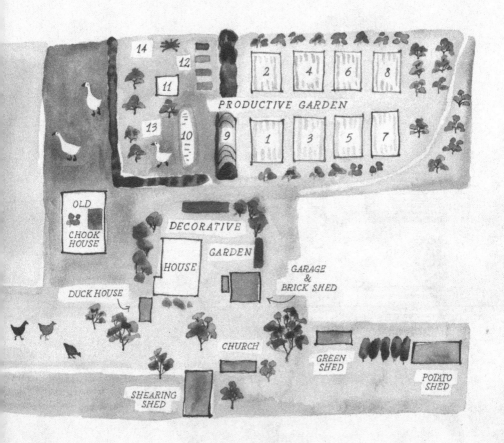

PRODUCTIVE GARDEN

1–8. GARDEN BLOCKS   12. COMPOST AREA

9. POLY TUNNEL   13. ORCHARD

10. GOOSE POND   14. BURN PILE

11. PIGEONNIER

How we got here

As I sit writing, I'm looking out at a landscape that shifts and changes daily. The air is perfectly still. The lake surrenders her reflections of the surrounding trees, with no distortion. The birds sing softly, observing the morning quietude. The goats, sheep and geese are all sorting out their positions in the paddock, as three juvenile kangaroos hop by, engrossed in their journey. At a glance, this could be seen as a perfect autumn morning.

But our world is changing, at an ever-increasing pace. We are living through a time when environmental catastrophes and disease stalk us all, no matter where we are. It is a time to take stock. I have been engaged in this process of evaluation for some years, trying to make decisions that allow me to step a great deal more gently on the earth. I am painfully aware that not all of us have the luxury of being able to make such choices and feel passionately that those who can, should. No matter how small a decision is, no matter how tiny its beneficial impact, all changes for the better could form a tsunami of positive differences and hope sweeping over the earth.

I have lived in country Victoria for more than half my life. After growing up in the peri-urban regions of Melbourne, I had a yearning in my twenties to change my inner-city existence to a more countrified one. As much as I loved the city and what it had to offer, the joy of a childhood spent playing in dirt and scrabbling over trees never left me. I wanted to plunge my hands into the dirt again.

In the early 1990s, a job came up in the Central Victorian town of Daylesford, and I jumped at it. It was a position working under

Alla Wolf-Tasker as head chef in her esteemed restaurant and small hotel, Lake House. I also bought a tiny workers' cottage high on a hill, overlooking the incongruously named Slum Dam. I had no concept at the time of what a life-changing decision it was. I was a bolshy, brash young city chef, thinking that it would be a chance to recapture the innocence of childhood, not understanding that time of my life was gone. A house, a mortgage and a completely new way of living announced the real start of my adult life, rather than heralding me reclaiming my childhood. I made the decision on the fly, with the surety that only the indomitable spirit of youth can provide. Have I ever been sorry I did it? No. I did try to relocate to the city at the turn of the century, but it was a disaster. Something about it made me sick, mentally and physically, and I came running 'home' to the country, to dirt under my fingernails and to the clear night skies.

That is not to say that living in the country was, or is, always bliss. When people first contemplate moving to the country, or talk about it with others, their vision is often of a pastoral life. This is a mistake.

The reality of living in a small country town was nothing that I, in my impetuous youth, had contemplated. It can be the worst of both worlds at times. You have a semi-suburban existence, yet with none of the abundance of a more urban life. Theatres, cinemas and even the choice of a variety of restaurants are usually a lengthy car trip away. The cost of owning a house and trying to renovate it was challenging for me. And yet ...

I learned patience and tolerance in spades in those early years in Daylesford. But it is the gardening that I remember the most. It had an indelible impact on me. That first house had an aspect that made it feel rural, and I spent many back-breaking years installing a beautiful English-style cottage garden – brush cutting blackberries away, to discover a babbling brook; repairing old stone walls; mowing, snipping, planting. I was also slowly doing up the tiny house, and then I sold it. I didn't really profit from the exercise financially, but something had taken hold of me.

I drifted in the country rental market for a few years, feeling a little aimless and always grieving the loss of my garden. In the early 2000s, I moved from Daylesford to Malmsbury, another Central Victorian town. I purchased my second run-down workers' cottage, on 0.2 hectares of land.

The years between owning a house in Daylesford and in Malmsbury were lean. I was racked by poor mental health, and that other hangover from youthful days: debt. I chose the house in Malmsbury simply because it was the cheapest on the market. A friend quipped that she hoped I had a lot of money, as she could see in it no redeeming features. She was right: it was truly awful. If it had been derelict, fixing it up would have been easier, but it had been fiddled with at some stage; aluminium windows had been installed, and nasty, cheap pine dado boards and a lot of homemade concreting had been added. The toilet and the bathroom may as well have been outside, they were so basic and uncomfortable. The kitchen barely existed. But to me, the house represented promise, safety and a new beginning.

A couple of years after I arrived in Malmsbury, life had improved somewhat. I had settled into my little house, started work on the garden and adjusted to living with the shortcomings of the building. Then, through a serious of serendipitous events, I was a restaurateur. I had seized the opportunity to take over an existing site in one of the historic buildings of the famed Piper Street in nearby Kyneton, opening a French bistrot-style restaurant. A little like my forays in the 1990s, this was more an impulse move than one done with great thought.

The next eight years would shape, in a profound way, the person I was to become. Several years after I started the restaurant, simply named Annie Smithers' Bistrot, I bought the quarter hectare adjoining my Malmsbury house. My grand land holding was now almost half a hectare. I wanted the extra land because I had a plan.

In 2001, Hugh Fearnley-Whittingstall released *The River Cottage Cookbook*. I have to confess that, to this day, I have never watched the television show that the book was based on. It wasn't until around 2004 that I purchased a copy on the recommendation of a friend. I bought it with a companion copy of the recently released *The Whole Beast: Nose to Tail Eating* by the ever-charming Fergus Henderson.

Those heady days of the turn of the century were summoning a very different approach to our food – both cooking and growing it. While Carlo Petrini had been pushing his slow food message in Italy since the mid-1980s, people in many other countries were starting to believe that food sovereignty, ethics and miles were all going to be defining questions in food culture in the following decades. On either side of the Atlantic, luminaries such as Alice Waters and Darina Allen were increasingly making noise about organics and forgotten techniques.

It was an incredibly exciting time to be a young restaurateur. Mr Fearnley-Whittingstall's book had a deep effect on me: it made me want to be a smallholder, preferably in the bucolic English countryside. He inspired a generation of people to plant apples, create vegetable gardens and spend an awful lot of money at nurseries. I am not sure how many he has inspired to kill chickens, raise and slaughter pigs, or slit the throat of an unfortunate sheep, but there are at least two highly regarded chefs in Tasmania pursuing lives that look very much inspired by the *River Cottage* model. I remember Mr Fearnley-Whittingstall's book entreating us all to do anything that would make a difference, even if it was as small as growing a tomato plant on a balcony. This resonated with me; I knew I wanted to be more connected to my food and where it came from – but, that said, I wasn't stung into action immediately. With a falling-down house, expanding land and a new business to tend, realising dreams of self-sufficiency needed money, time and commitment, all of which were in very short supply back then.

But by 2008, I was ready for action. Restaurant life had settled down, my house was well on the way to being far more habitable, and I had adjusted to the idea that perhaps Malmsbury was going to be my forever home. I had all but forsaken the notion that, one day, I would grow up and be able to afford real acreage. If this were to be my lot, I'd jolly well better make it as perfect for me as I possibly could.

That house and little bit of land would become my idiosyncratic statement about the rage I felt at how the world was changing around me. I would grow food, I would keep chickens and bees, and I would try to tread more carefully on the earth than I had before.

It is important to remember that the world was very different in 2008. It was in that year, in July, that the first smartphone was introduced into Australia. While the World Wide Web had been functioning in its current form for several years, it was still my habit first to consult reference books and then spend my evenings looking at the internet for inspiration.

I had never lost sight of the ideas Hugh had planted, but I now had the mental space to return to them and read many other 'homesteading' books. I could also delve into the early web presence of the many American sites that promised huge hauls of food from modest allotments.

I was also keenly aware that, historically, the land immediately around my cottage would have been used to feed the family of seven that lived under its tiny roof. I was in an area that had had excellent Country Women's Association representation; yet, in my lifetime, all the knowledge of self-sufficiency that would have been everyday had seemingly been lost. Throughout my years at school, through the 1970s and 1980s, even living on the urban fringe as I did and enjoying being on a couple of hectares, we never considered growing our own food. And though my mother was an excellent cook, who entertained frequently, food was purchased at the local shops and supermarket, and there was never a sense that we had to prepare for tomorrow today. Seasonality was drifting away from us even then. Without ever noticing, I had lived in an area where all the historic orchards were bulldozed to make way for large houses – houses so large that they filled almost all the land they were on, except for the space reserved for a pool or a tennis court. There was not a compost heap or raised garden bed to be seen. Nor was it ever mentioned, not even once, that farming might be a viable job for us when we were adults. It was seemingly a vocation consigned on a hereditary principle: if you came from a farm, you stayed on the farm.

I ruminated on all this in Malmsbury and realised that I had little to no idea of how to grow food. While the desire was definitely there, I still had to face the uncomfortable truth that my time to upskill was limited, so I employed a gardener, Simon Rickard. The first six months he was with me, we confined the 'test' garden to a small plot of about 5 square metres in the backyard. The area had been created by beautiful stone walls at the back of the house. After turning over the soil in that area, we saw clearly that the site represented self-sufficiency from the preceding decades. We would keep turning up bones: mainly large leg bones from cattle. It transpired later, with some terrible results, that we were starting our small-scale vegetable growing on a site where meat had been preserved in the past. We deduced from the amount of salt that came to the surface of the soil after heavy rains that saltpetre, a home preserving agent long since replaced by the use of nitrates, was present in the area. This meant that our first forays were not entirely successful, as there were issues with pH, salt and drainage; yet, the defeats taught us valuable lessons.

And whatever the failures at hand, the desire to grow food had taken root. I wanted, more than ever, to become more proactive about growing things for the restaurant, as well as for myself.

After our first disasters, in the autumn of Simon's first year, I bought a small tractor and we ripped up a paddock that was to become my vegetable garden and orchard for the next nine years. Those years were fuller than I could ever have conceived. Abundant harvests of gorgeous fruits and vegetables, epic failures, flooding, pestilence, and an overriding sense of achievement. No matter how hard those times could be, there was learning, passion and devotion, all in the pursuit of one of life's basics: the careful growing of food for sustenance.

When I sold the house in Malmsbury after fourteen years, it was unrecognisable. It had been lovingly restored, and the garden was a picture of productivity. There were over thirty-five producing fruit trees, all chosen for their various roles in the kitchen, of eating, cooking, preserving. One area held cane fruit, strawberries and asparagus. Fifteen 22-metre rows produced fruit, vegetables and salad all year round. A series of chookyards enabled me to keep different breeds of chickens and geese. There was a small hothouse for raising seeds, growing micro herbs and protecting plants from frost. And there was a darling little storehouse, rebuilt on the foundations of the old milking shed, that was specifically designed to store fruit and root vegetables in a traditional manner. The original square bed had been planted out as a joyous perennial display that brought me great delight, whatever the season, as I looked out my kitchen window.

The agony of those first attempts forgotten quickly, I had an enormous sense of pride in how my time and energy were spent in those years. There would always be a peppering of disappointments, but I grew accustomed to dealing with them. I had turned my land into a productive garden that supplied up to 90 per cent of the restaurant's fruit and vegetables. I had also gone some way to transforming my semi-suburban country existence into one that felt much more rural, simply due to the way the land was utilised. I was living many people's dream, and certainly mine, albeit on a small piece of land.

Then romance intervened. I met Susan. My little bachelor fiefdom in Malmsbury was never going to be big enough for me, her and her two daughters. If we were to live together, it would mean starting again somewhere new. We began to hunt for a place.

In a perfect world, I am sure, real estate investments would be made with the head, not the heart. But I often wonder how frequently that happens, especially when it comes to buying country properties.

While I had spent the best part of a quarter of a century in the country, and no matter how hard I tried to dismiss it, there was always something scratching at the back of my mind. I wanted more – not too much more, but more. Two, maybe 4, or even 8, hectares. A long driveway, rolling hills, a dam or two. Maybe some outbuildings, or maybe just a beautiful plot of land that I could plonk an architectural marvel on. The dreamscape is always so safe: it contains no realities of the day-to-day existence of a working farm, especially one that is vital to the main part of your life, in which you are already a little stretched. There is no concept of the vortex it can create; just a happy reverie.

There was a lot going on at this time. I had exchanged the bigger restaurant for a smaller one in the small country town of Trentham, around 30 kilometres from Malmsbury. The new restaurant was tiny, with a small staff and a fixed menu, and was run according to the most sustainable practices I could manage. All those years of experience had distilled to a business that wasted no food, no staff hours and no resources.

The task at hand was to find the ideal property: one that a newly blended family of a couple of fifty-year-olds and two adolescent children could call home for many years to come, and where we could carve out the most sustainable existence possible. After many false starts, we finally found 'the one'. It was outside our budget, but completely inside our dreamscape: just over 9 hectares of land, with 34 megalitres of spring-fed water, numerous sheds and outbuildings, exceptional soil and a landscape reminiscent of a Capability Brown garden. We became the custodians of Babbington Park, and together embarked on a quest to live more sustainably and gently.

42 HIGH ST

du Fermier

OPEN FOR LUNC
FRIDAY - MONDAY

RESERVATIONS ESSENT
PHONE 03 5424 1634

The restaurant

AHHH, DU FERMIER. The little restaurant with a name that is particularly bad Franglais. It is touted as meaning 'from the farmhouse' but, in fact, translates to 'of the farmer' – a bastardisation of grammar and poor translation that only a non-French speaker could come up with. Despite starting with the handicap of an imperfect moniker, du Fermier operates in a way that very few restaurants can. It's in a small regional town, with a population a nick over 1200. We waste virtually no food, people hours or wine. It has become a model for having a minimal footprint – more through a series of random choices, conscious and unconscious, than by design.

How did du Fermier evolve into what it is today?

There was nothing planned about it. My dear friend Cynthia came to me with a proposition: she had a shop in Trentham, the tenants were on the move, and would I consider having a second outpost there? I thought, not for long, and plunged headlong into it. Trentham is located between Kyneton and Daylesford, thus straddling the two regions I had spent so much time cooking in. A small town, away from the main roads, with a quintessential charming-village feel. I felt that it suited my love for provincial French cuisine, where the simplicity of both the village and the food style melds into something incredibly special.

First came the name and then the concept. The name needed to represent the path that I had been treading, cooking directly from what my 'little' farm produced. In its first incarnation, it was a cafe-come-homewares/produce store that a local couple ran for me. Over the twelve months that I oversaw both the restaurant in Kyneton and the smaller Trentham one, it had become clear that I was not suited to running multiple venues. I needed to be hands-on.

After eight years in Kyneton, the lure of du Fermier's smaller, simpler building and business became very strong. The departure of my staff meant that the Trentham building sat idle for a few months while I sold the bigger restaurant in Kyneton. Then, one fine May day, I arrived, to hang my shingle in a new town.

I had not left Kyneton in completely sound mind. While I had sold the restaurant for a fair price, it had become obvious to me that, in an attempt to do better by the world, I had expected way too much of my restaurant financially. The cost of farming my own fruit and vegetables over a period of years had averaged out at $50 per kilogram, and the major component of that was labour. This was not only the labour involved in the actual growing of the food but also the increased work in sorting, washing and grading the produce. All was compounded by running an à la carte menu in Kyneton, which meant food often got thrown away. This is heartbreaking when you have known that food from when it was a seed. Heartbreaking when it has cost you $50 per kilo. Heartbreaking when you realise that, while trying to do the right thing, you are plunging headlong into financial ruin. Most of the bills were paid by the time of my departure, save one: a hefty bill to the tax department.

The experience had rocked my ideals, left me broken and unsure. I wanted to reinvent du Fermier so it would be as compact as possible: a smaller, less complicated business to run. I didn't want it to be a restaurant; I wanted it to be a cafe. I wanted a simpler life.

My recollections of that time are a little hazy – squashed back somewhere, so I don't have to remember the dual pressures of immense debt and extreme tiredness. Du Fermier had to make money, but I didn't want to charge patrons too much. It was open for breakfast and lunch four days a week and for dinner two nights a week; I was cooking in the kitchen on my own. It was a brutal existence. At this stage, du Fermier was run to achieve one purpose: to pay down the tax debt.

In the notes on my phone from those days is the original menu concept:

Breakfast

Toast

Fruit toast

Croissant

Granola

Eggs, scrambled, fried, poached

Sides: Bacon, tomato, mushroom, spinach,

salmon, hash browns

Corn fritters, roasted tomatoes, bacon

Livers, spinach, bacon, veal jus

French toast

Waffles

Pancakes with maple syrup and pure cream

Its simplicity belies the amount of work that was involved for one person in the kitchen and, on top of this, I insisted on making bread not only for the customers but for a menu du jour on Friday and Saturday nights. The idea was for a French-style cafe using farm-fresh produce. A night-time menu looked a little like this:

A sample dinner menu

Buckwheat crepes with ham and Gruyère and salad

Braised lamb with garlic and rosemary and spiced white beans

Pears in red wine, custard, walnut brittle and langue de chat

It was a hard time. While there were a lot of laughs, there was a lot of chaos and, if you listen to a staff member who is still with me, a version of Annie who has since been banished: 'Shouty Annie'.

Still, after a few months, the tax debt was retired. We had fiddled with du Fermier's hours a little by then; we dropped the Thursday service, and our new sense of fiscal freedom gave us the chance to retire breakfast.

This was not the only change that had been underway – my concept of having a simple cafe had also been put to bed. Over those months, it became apparent that the customers didn't want me to fill baguettes and toast sandwiches; they wanted me to continue cooking French brasserie–style food, and they wanted the set menu that was offered at night to be offered during the day. We had morphed into a place that had a small three-by-three-by-three à la carte menu and a menu du jour, similar to something that you would find on the continent.

Lunch

Soup

Baguette pork schnitzel, beetroot/cabbage slaw

Omelette, fries, salad

Charcuterie

Ham crepes

A quail wrapped in prosciutto, pan-fried and served on salad

Grilled steak sandwich, red capsicum relish, greens, bacon

Pan-fried blue eye, red peppers, Nicola potatoes and saffron

Confit duck leg, potato sarladaise and green beans

Braised beef, shallots, bacon, mushrooms on mash

Handcut fries

Green salad

Passionfruit syrup cake

Salted chocolate chip and thyme biscuit

Doughnut

Danish

Chocolate mousse

Coffee éclair

Mille-feuille with pastry cream and raspberries

Apple frangipani tart

When we stopped breakfast, there was a great torrent of outcry. The complaints opened my eyes to a very valuable realisation: you cannot be everything to everybody. Someone was always wanting something more, something different, and hospitality is about making people happy. As professionals, we always strive to overdeliver, often to our own detriment. We are in the business of saying yes, so the decision to say no was not made lightly.

Stability reigned for two years, with us offering lunch Friday to Sunday, and dinner Friday and Saturday. I was able to spend more time in the garden growing our food, doing a little writing and holding my eponymous cooking classes. Writing about food was becoming more and more of a joy for me, and I was lucky enough to be commissioned to write both for a newspaper and an excellent publisher.

The classes were a completely different kettle of fish, though no less rewarding. I discovered that I loved teaching and sharing my knowledge, and found a perfect stage for this in running demonstration cooking courses. They essentially distilled the practice I had from completing kitchen tasks hundreds, sometimes thousands, of times into lively lessons where that knowledge was spread among enthralled participants.

As well, Cynthia sold me du Fermier's building. That made it feel like I'd be staying put forever. That year, 2016, I turned fifty. There was no denying that my body was tiring after thirty-three years of working at a stove, and the seventeen-hour days were getting tough to recover from. We were nearly always booked out, we grew most of the fruit and vegetables that we used, and I realised that I wanted to grow food and cook in the long term. To do that, I had to make it personally sustainable. I could no longer do the extra-long shifts. Something had to give.

Strangely enough, as I have always preferred working during the day, I chose to stick with doing dinner. Then, without giving any real notice, we axed dinner and added Monday lunch. It was risky, substituting a lunch at the start of the week for the two most profitable services, but I was tired and it was time to make the restaurant suit me, not everybody else. It was also a decision that had been made on a reverse-engineered fiscal policy. I was locking myself into making a finite amount of money. Over the years, I had tried hunting the dollar, and it didn't work for me.

Some years later, when I was hosting a culinary trip to Gascony, we had lunch at a workers' cafe. It was a simple affair: ridiculously inexpensive and run by one woman in the kitchen. In the moment I chatted to this cafe's lovely owner/cook, I realised that I had achieved a version of the dream I had imagined for myself. There was a similar thread of authenticity between my place and hers, and it made me smile both inside and out.

Fifteen years in two restaurants has been a wild ride. For a long time, becoming more self-sustaining in my food production was calculated as an expense that thwarted the financial viability of my business. When I stopped thinking of it as a negative and accepted that it was as necessary as power or gas, I absorbed the cost and now view it as just part of my basic infrastructure.

Over these past years, in making the restaurant work for me, as opposed to me working for it, I have become a great champion of the old Labour Day principles of eight/eight/eight. After all these years in the hospitality industry, working twelve/fifteen/eighteen-hour days, I delight in the ability to use my time away from work however I see fit. I now refuse to condemn anyone to the stultified life that comes from working too much. Everyone who works with me has a right to their life: in employing them, I don't own them.

The concept of waste has become far broader for me. Sustainability is more than making sure that you don't let vegetables rot in the crisper, and endeavouring to use everything; it is about how and what you choose to waste. On a personal level, I waste time constantly, idly, but to waste someone else's is not sustainable. Re-use, re-work, simplify. The great joy of not having much to start with is that you have little to lose. It also creates an environment where creative solutions can often be found.

Favourite recipes from all phases of du Fermier

This is a collection of recipes that illustrate the many phases of du Fermier. Over the years, hundreds of different dishes have been executed for all manner of occasions. Some are my personal triumphs; others are ones that the customers have loved the most.

Breakfast

Croissants

I have made my own croissants since I was a little girl. It started as a Christmas breakfast tradition, and I have been working away at my technique ever since. I have always adhered to the wonderful Julia Child's recipe from *Mastering the Art of French Cooking, Vol. 2.*

A few years ago, I began to feel that my croissants were not living up to the expectations of what a modern croissant should look like. The layering was not obvious enough, the crunch not pronounced enough. On Instagram, I happened across a wonderful baker from England and have adapted his recipe for my own use. So, thank you to Adam Pagor of Grain & Hearth for allowing me to share this recipe.

MAKES 12

425 g bread flour
10 g salt
40 g caster sugar
135 ml warm milk
135 ml warm water
10 g instant yeast
250 g unsalted butter
1 egg

Mix the flour, salt and sugar together in a bowl. Combine the milk and water and warm to blood temperature. Add the yeast, mix lightly and let sit for 5 minutes to activate the yeast. Add the wet ingredients to the dry and mix with the paddle, if using a stand mixer, or your hands. Mix until it comes together into a smooth dough; knead for about 5 minutes. Put in a lightly oiled bowl, cover and refrigerate overnight.

Next morning, remove the butter from the refrigerator 20–30 minutes before you want to work with it. Take the dough out, flatten into a rectangle, which will remove the gas, and place in the freezer while you shape the butter.

Cut a piece of baking paper about 30 × 30 cm. Place the butter in the middle and whack it with a rolling pin until it is in a rectangle about 15 × 10 cm. Fold the paper around so you can force it into the corners to make a nice even rectangle. Freeze for about 5 minutes. Remove both the dough and the butter from the freezer and roll the dough out into a rectangle about 30 × 15 cm. Unwrap the butter and place in the middle, bring the sides in to cover the butter, and pinch-seal the edges. Turn it 90° and roll out again to 45 cm, fold in three (what's known as a single fold), turn 90° and roll out to 45 cm again, fold in three, wrap and chill in the freezer for 15–20 minutes. Each time you roll it out, you can trim the ends square and lay the scraps on the sheet to be reincorporated into the dough. After resting the dough, remove from the freezer and repeat the process, rolling the block out to a 45-cm sheet and folding in three. Place back in the freezer for 20 minutes. Now it is time to roll the sheet out to cut the croissants. Roll into a rectangle about 45 × 20 cm. Trim the edges and cut into 12 triangles, docking the middle of the bottom of the triangle to facilitate rolling. Line a couple of trays with baking paper. Stretch or roll the point out and roll the croissant up; place on the tray point side down. Repeat until all rolled. Cover with a tea towel and place in a warm spot until doubled in size (2–3 hours).

Preheat the oven to 180 °C, with a little baking dish of hot water in the bottom of the oven to create a bit of steam. Make an egg wash by beating the egg with a good pinch of salt and a dash of water. Brush the croissants gently with the egg wash; I like to give them 2 coats. Place in the oven and bake for 15–20 minutes until golden. Remove the croissants to a rack and rest them for a few minutes before eating. They are also perfectly good when reheated for a few minutes the next morning or frozen and reheated.

Granola

I love a good granola, and this one used to feature on our breakfast menu, with fresh poached fruit or berries and yoghurt. In later incarnations, it has also been bagged up and sold on our jam counter. The mix can be varied to suit personal taste. This quantity makes a large jar full: just over half a kilo's worth. Given that I like to eat a bowlful and others just like to sprinkle it on fruit and yoghurt, determining portions is difficult.

40 g coconut oil, butter or vegetable oil, etc.

120 ml honey or maple syrup

1 tsp flaked salt

340 g rolled oats or mix of oats, rye flakes, barley,
    puffed quinoa, etc.

200 g nuts, chopped (I use flaked almonds)

50 g pumpkin seeds

50 g sesame seeds

50 g coconut shavings

½ tsp cinnamon

100 g dried fruit (I use currants and cranberries)

Preheat the oven to 150 °C. Line a large baking tray with baking paper.

Heat the fat and syrup together until combined and liquid.

Add all dry ingredients, except dried fruit, to the baking tray. Mix. Add the warm syrup, stir through the dry ingredients. Bake at 150 °C for 30–40 minutes or until golden, stirring 3 or 4 times.

Remove from the oven, stir in the fruit, cool. Keep in a sealed container.

Pain perdu

Something unfortunate happened to 'lost bread', the literal translation of pain perdu, when it became the ubiquitous French toast served hither and yon. It seems to have morphed into the very worst version of itself (a little like the fate of the quiche Lorraine that follows). This is a beautiful version that is perfect for breakfast but also stands up to being served as a dessert. The sifting of flour and sugar over the soaked bread adds a delicious caramelised crispness to the finished result.

SERVES 2

For the custard

100 ml milk

150 ml thickened cream

2 large eggs

3 tbsp sugar

1 tbsp Armagnac

1 tsp vanilla essence

For the pain perdu

2 slices good white bread (sliced 3 cm thick)

1 tbsp caster sugar

1 tbsp plain flour

2 tbsp unsalted butter

To make the custard for the pain perdu, whisk together the milk, cream, eggs, sugar, Armagnac and vanilla essence until the mixture is combined.

Place the bread in a deep dish or tray that is just large enough to hold the bread in a single layer and cover with the custard. If your dish is too large, the custard won't soak into the bread completely. If you don't have a suitable dish, you can use a sealable plastic bag and press out the excess air. Cover and refrigerate for a day, turning the bread over a few times.

Preheat the oven to 230°C. Remove the soaked pain perdu from the refrigerator and flip one more time. Mix 1 tbsp of sugar with 1 tbsp of flour and sprinkle half the mixture on the tops of the bread, using a small sieve to ensure the flour gets sprinkled evenly.

Add the butter to a cast-iron frying pan, or other heavy pan, and heat over medium heat.

When the butter has melted and the foaming subsides, add the bread, flour-sprinkled side down, and fry for about 5 minutes.

Dust the pain perdu with the remaining flour/sugar mixture and check that the underside is well browned. Be careful that your heat is not up too high or it will burn; if it looks like it's browning too quickly, turn the heat down.

Flip the bread over and put the pan in the oven.

Bake for 8–10 minutes. Keep a close eye on it, as the sugar will burn easily. You want the surface of your pain perdu to be very dark but not burned, and then it will have a delicious crunch.

Light lunch

Quiche Lorraine

I have a bit of an obsession with making the perfect quiche. I abhor the leathery, soggy-pastry version that seems to proliferate in Australian bakeries. For me, the ideal quiche is one with deep golden pastry, perfectly cooked onions and bacon, and a deep silken custard also cooked to perfection. The only recipe that I have ever used is Elizabeth David's.

SERVES 6
1 quantity shortcrust pastry
1 small onion, finely diced
6 thin rashers streaky bacon, cut into lardons
300 ml cream
3 egg yolks
1 egg
salt and pepper

Preheat the oven to 200 °C. Blind bake the tart shells. Reduce heat to 160 °C. Sweat the onion in a frying pan in a little oil until soft. Add the bacon and cook for another couple of minutes. Arrange these on the pastry. Mix the cream and eggs, then season with a tiny bit of salt and lots of freshly ground black pepper. Pour into the pastry-lined tin and put in the oven. Cook for 40 minutes if a large quiche or for about 12 minutes if you're making small ones. The filling will puff up and turn golden brown. Let it rest for a minute or two when out of the oven, then serve. It's good at room temperature too, but don't eat it cold from the fridge.

Ham and cheese crepes

An adaptable favourite of mine for lunch, served with a crisp green salad dressed with a sharp vinaigrette. I love the combination of ham, Gruyère and Dijon mustard, but they can also be filled with a sauté of mushrooms and spinach and Gruyère, or blanched asparagus, Gruyère and Dijon mustard.

SERVES 4–6
4 tbsp Dijon mustard
250 g sliced leg ham
250 g Gruyère, grated

For the buckwheat crepes
500 ml milk
3 large eggs
80 g unsalted butter, melted
70 g buckwheat flour
105 g plain flour
¼ tsp sea salt
a little extra butter

Whisk milk, eggs and melted butter together. Place the flours and salt in a bowl, make a well in the centre and whisk in the liquid ingredients. Whisk until you have a smooth batter. Cover and chill overnight.

To fry the crepes, remove the batter from the refrigerator about an hour before. Stir it briskly; it should be the consistency of heavy cream. If it is too thick, dilute with a little more milk.

Heat a 22-cm cast-iron or non-stick pan on the stovetop.

Drop a tiny piece of butter into the hot pan and swirl it about. Lift the pan and pour ¼ cup of the batter into the middle of the hot skillet, swirling the pan to distribute the batter quickly and evenly. The pan shouldn't be too hot or too cold: the batter should start cooking within a few seconds, giving you just enough time to swirl it.

After about a minute, run a non-stick spatula around the underside of the rim of the crepe, then flip the crepe over. Let the crepe cook on the flip side for about 30 seconds, then slide it out onto a cooling rack. Repeat, cooking the crepes with the remaining batter, stirring the batter every so often as you go.

For the bechamel
30 g butter, chopped
40 g plain flour
550 ml milk
40 g parmesan cheese, finely grated
¼ tsp salt
a good pinch of ground nutmeg

Melt the butter in a medium saucepan over medium-high heat until foaming. Add flour. Cook, stirring, for 1–2 minutes or until bubbling. Remove from heat. Slowly add the milk, whisking constantly, until the mixture is smooth. Return to heat. Cook, stirring with a wooden spoon, for 10–12 minutes or until the sauce comes to the boil, thickens and coats the back of a wooden spoon. Remove from heat. Stir in parmesan, salt and nutmeg.

Preheat the oven to 180°C.

Butter a baking dish that will hold 16 rolled crepes.

Spread a little Dijon on each crepe, and on top of it some ham and a sprinkle of grated Gruyère. Make sure you leave some grated cheese for the top. Arrange the crepes snugly in the baking dish, smear the bechamel over the top, and then scatter with cheese. Bake for about 20 minutes until golden brown. Serve with a crisp green salad.

Main course–style dishes for lunch or dinner

Confit duck leg

I cook an enormous amount of duck at the restaurant. It delights me, in that I can use every skerrick of the gutted bird: rendering the fat, making sausages from the neck skin, using all the bones for stock, and treating the legs and the breasts to multiple cooking techniques. But my favourite is a good basic confit, where the leg has been salted and then cooked slowly in rendered fat – an age-old preservation technique from France. I love it served simply with sautéed potatoes, green beans and a sharply dressed salad.

SERVES 4
4 duck legs
1 tbsp flaked salt
4 sprigs thyme
1 bay leaf
1 garlic clove, crushed
500 g rendered duck fat

Lay the duck legs flesh side up in a non-reactive baking tray, either glass or stainless steel, and sprinkle with the salt, thyme, bay leaf and garlic. Cover with cling wrap and leave to marinate in the fridge overnight. The next day, rinse off and pat dry with a cloth.

Preheat the oven to 140 °C. Melt the duck fat over low heat. Place legs skin side up in a baking dish that has them very snugly packed, and cover with the melted fat. Place in the oven and cook for about 2½ hours until the duck legs are very tender. Remove from the oven, leave them to cool in their fat and refrigerate.

When you are ready to use the legs, either reheat in a non-stick pan over low heat till the flesh is warmed through and the skin crisp, or in an oven preheated to 190 °C in a pan or baking dish.

Spiced lamb shanks with quince

Braising is a well-used piece of weaponry in my arsenal of cooking techniques. It is a process where the long, slow cooking of meat in a covered dish turns tough meat and connective tissue into soft, gelatinous deliciousness. This recipe for lamb shanks and quinces is French–Moroccan inspired.

SERVES 4

4 lamb shanks
salt and pepper
1 tbsp olive oil
large knob butter
2 large onions, halved then cut into wedges
4 garlic cloves, crushed
4 strips zest from 1 lemon, plus the juice
2 tsp ground cinnamon
2 tsp ground coriander

1 tsp ground ginger
1 tsp ground cumin
a good pinch of saffron strands
1 heaped tbsp tomato puree
1 tbsp clear honey
400 ml good lamb or beef stock
2 quinces, peeled, quartered and cored

Preheat the oven to 230 °C. Season the shanks with a little salt and pepper and the oil, then place in a baking dish and brown in the oven for 10 minutes, or until dark golden all over, turning them once.

Meanwhile, in a casserole dish or large pan, melt the butter. Soften the onions for 10 minutes on a medium heat until golden, then add the garlic. Remove shanks from the oven and turn it down to 160 °C.

Add the strips of lemon zest and spices to the onion pan. Cook for 1 minute, then stir in the tomato puree, honey, stock and half the lemon juice. Bring to a simmer and then pour over the shanks in the baking tray. Arrange the quince quarters in and around the meat. Then cover with a lid or a layer of aluminium foil and braise in the oven for 2 hours.

Remove the lid or foil, return the tray to the oven and cook for 30 minutes more. Spoon away any excess fat. The sauce will be fairly thin, so if you prefer a thicker stew, remove the lamb and quinces to a serving plate, then boil the cooking juices until thickened. Season, add the lemon juice and serve with the lamb. This goes beautifully with some fluffy couscous or a rice pilaf and crisp green salad.

If you love the idea of this recipe, and while you are going to the trouble of a long braise and want to extend it to another meal, this is also an excellent base for a fabulous soup. Multiply all the ingredients by half again, and cook as per the recipe. Strip the meat from the extra two shanks and reserve some of the cooking juices. Dilute with stock till it has the consistency of thick soup; add a tin of cooked chickpeas and some roasted pumpkin pieces. Adjust the seasoning and serve with grilled flatbread and a dollop of yoghurt.

A dessert or two

Concorde cake

This funny French creation was invented by pastry chef Gaston Lenôtre in 1969 to celebrate the first flights of the Concorde aeroplane. The blowzy chocolate confection makes me giggle because it always reminds me of an over-the-top bathing cap and seems to have nothing in common with the beautiful sleek lines of the plane it was named after. That said, it has a certain *je ne sais quoi* and is a good choice for a dinner party, as the components can be made the day before and assembled on the day you wish to serve it. Even though the Concorde cake is meringue-based, it is not too sweet.

SERVES 8

For the meringue
50 g Dutch cocoa powder
160 g icing sugar
9 egg whites
220 g caster sugar

For the chocolate mousse
240 g dark (55%) chocolate,
    broken into pieces
150 g unsalted butter
4 egg yolks
6 egg whites
2 tbsp caster sugar

Preheat the oven to 150°C and line a large baking tray with baking paper.

To make the meringue, sift together the cocoa and icing sugar. In a stand mixer, whip the egg whites to stiff peaks, then add 1 tbsp caster sugar and beat in. Add the remaining caster sugar in batches, then gently fold in the cocoa mixture.

Scoop the meringue into a piping bag fitted with a plain nozzle and pipe 3 × 18-cm rounds onto the prepared tray. Pipe the rest in strips (the length doesn't matter as you will be breaking them up later). Place in the oven and bake for 1 hour. Turn off the oven and allow the meringues to cool in it with the door propped open.

To make the chocolate mousse, melt the chocolate and butter in a heatproof bowl set over a saucepan of barely simmering water. Stir until smooth and well combined, then whisk in the egg yolks. Whip the egg whites to soft peaks, then beat in the caster sugar. Gently fold the whites into the chocolate mixture, then cover and refrigerate until needed.

To assemble, spread a thin layer of mousse (about a quarter of it) on each meringue disc and place on top of each other. Seal the edge with the remaining mousse. Decorate the top and side with the broken strips of meringue. Sift icing sugar and cocoa over the cake if you wish to decorate it further.

Present it whole, then cut into wedges and serve with whipped cream.

Tarte Tatin

The simplicity of this tart is what makes it so special. We grow a particular apple to make it: Calville Blanc d'Hiver. This apple has a balsa wood–type texture with the capacity to hold its shape yet absorb the golden toffee. I always use the best-quality butter puff pastry for this tart.

SERVES 4

1 piece puff pastry, to cut a 20-cm round from

1 cup sugar

2 × ½ cup water

60 g unsalted butter

6–8 apples

Select a suitable shallow ovenproof dish. We like to use a copper tarte Tatin tin.

Cut the pastry in a round to cover the top with about 1 cm spare.

Preheat the oven to 220 °C.

To make the toffee, combine sugar and ½ cup water in a heavy-bottomed saucepan and stir over heat until sugar is dissolved. Boil until the toffee is a rich amber colour, remove from heat and carefully add the other ½ cup water and the butter. Whisk to combine.

Pour enough toffee into the ovenproof dish to coat the bottom. Keep the rest of the toffee mix for later. Peel the apples, cut them into quarters, remove the cores and then cut into eighths. Arrange the apple in the dish in concentric circles. Place the pastry on top, bake for approx. 20 minutes until the pastry is golden brown. Check to see if the apples are cooked; if not, reduce oven temperature to 180 °C and cook until the apples are soft. The time to cook will depend on the water content and variety of the apples. Remove from the oven, and cool the tart a little.

To serve, invert the tart onto serving plates and drizzle with some leftover caramel if you feel the apples have absorbed too much of the original amount.

Land

BABBINGTON PARK IS nestled on the outskirts of the tiny hamlet of Lyonville, 100 kilometres north-west of Melbourne.

Lyonville is on the southern-most border of the land of the Dja Dja Wurrung clans, or the Jaara people – one of five language groups that make up the Kulin nation that has inhabited southern Victoria for an estimated 40,000 years at least. Their way of life follows the seasons and works with the differences in landscape and climate of their Country, treading with care and respect on the earth. There are at least sixteen main clans of the Jaara people, each with their own niche across Country.

For me, the Loddon River highlights the importance of our environmental responsibilities on this land. Known by many names in the languages of her people, she is a vast waterway that travels 392 kilometres and descends nearly 570 metres along the way. She cleaves the Dja Dja Wurrung Country in two; I can only imagine how magnificent she was once, before the white man came and plundered her. It gives me great pause for thought that our practices impact on this river, and we will endeavour to do the best by her that we can.

Lyonville rests quietly in the south-western extremes of the Great Dividing Range, a land littered with the remnants of little volcanos. Our closest is Babbington Hill, a modest 820 metres above sea level. The old volcanic activity and the altitude have created an area rich in spring water, and it is springs running from underneath our property and our neighbours' land that form the head of the Loddon River.

In 2016, I had the great pleasure of sitting with a Jaara elder at a function. She told me beautiful stories of their two moiety ancestors, Bunjil the eagle and Waa the crow. Bunjil is a creator; Waa is in charge of the winds. The stories she told stayed with me, and when we arrived at Lyonville, I had cause to think on them every day. The winds can be ferocious here at Babbington, the crows are ever present, cawing at us as we pass, and our resident eagles swoop and soar above, occasionally dropping down to try to take a goose, always reminding us that we have no real claim to this land.

In the 1830s, New South Wales Surveyor General Thomas Mitchell was sent south. The European settlers were experiencing drought conditions and Mitchell's quest was to discover more arable land: Victoria. With the vast fertile plains of the Western District, the cool volcanic country drifting away from the Great Dividing Range, plus vast stands of hardwood forests and gold, Victoria held a wealth of new possibilities. On a local level, James Lyon and Richard Babbington seized vast chunks of the district in the early 1860s. In the years between Mitchell's and Lyon's arrivals, the settlers carried out a campaign of murder and mayhem – and spread pernicious European diseases – that decimated the Dja Dja Wurrung people. The possums flourished, as they were no longer hunted for pelts and food. The eagles and crows soared far above the desolation below, and a new era of white colonisation of central Victoria began.

The period from 1860 saw forty years of white colonisers' financial success, and the devastation of the local forests. The gold rush that started in the early 1850s in Ballarat and Bendigo, and the building boom in Melbourne, meant there was a great need for hardwood timber. Timber was required for buildings and for goldmine shafts, and much of it came from the forests that once grew across these volcanic regions. The forest around Lyonville was particularly magnificent – a towering old-growth, cool-climate forest, boasting many eucalypts, and messmate, peppermint, manna gum, candlebark and swamp gums. These were augmented by wattles, she-oaks and black-woods, all with an understorey of grasses, ferns and wildflowers, and a prodigious bird and native mammal population: birds of prey, right down to tiny wrens and marsupial mice, and right up to kangaroos. Almost certainly, at the foot of our hill, the quiet head of the Loddon housed platypi. A veritable cornucopia of Australian fauna and flora.

By 1884, there were three dozen mills operating in the area, which caused it to be termed a 'ruined forest' only sixty years from when Mitchell surveyed the area. And with the destruction of the trees would have come the decimation of flora and fauna, and of the First Peoples' land and way of life. For me, this illustrates how quickly irrevocable change can be inflicted on a landscape. In the span of an adult life, an old-growth forest region was reduced to ruined forest status. Knowing the history of this small part of the country, I'm more keen than ever to try to find a better way to live on this land, and encourage others to live more carefully on theirs.

The decline of the timber and milling industries set the local settler community on a path of agricultural pursuits. The settlers of this region were mainly from the United Kingdom, and they seemed to gather in groups of, for example, Irish, English and Scottish. Trentham is still known for its strong connections to its Irish Catholic roots, yet Lyonville had a much more Cornish flavour. The cleared land was deep, rich volcanic soil. There was an abundance of water and a very English climate. At altitudes of over 700 metres, it was also a very cold area. It is no wonder that there was an influx of Cornish people. The mining minds of many Cornish men would have been fired by the thought of unimaginable riches in the Australian gold-fields; and, if they became disillusioned with their finds, the men were able to drift into other work, such as with timber, and then farming.

The Botheras family and their relatives farmed the land where Babbington Park now stands for over fifty years. Fred Botheras's line extended back to Cornwall. His forefather Thomas (born 1837) emigrated to Australia in 1856, and he died in nearby Bullarto in 1892. The family farmed extensively around Bullarto and Lyonville for over a century. Fred was the last of the Botheras family to farm this patch, eventually admitting it was too much for him as he got older, and calling on his niece to help out. She and her husband and family, the Collings, then managed the farm for more than ten years before it was subdivided and sold off in the early 21st century.

Before its subdivision, the farm was a little more than 80 acres (32.4 hectares), and was what is known as a mixed farm. Potatoes were grown, sheep and cattle were run, and other agricultural crops, both cash crops and feed crops, were sown.

Across the gully, the Bremner family have been growing organic vegetables since settling there in 1890. The farming practices of both the Bremners and the Botheras have huge implications for me 130 years later. The use of natural growing techniques has meant that the insidious insecticide dieldrin was not used on these pastures. Dieldrin has a very long half-life and would have impacted our operations a great deal; thankfully, none is present. At one stage in the 1990s, the farm had organic certification for its potato and corn crops. These careful practices by generations of farmers have preserved the land at a level better than most.

For me, there is always the correlation of the small farm to the small restaurant. When you have a limited canvas to work with to provide your income, there is no room for waste or negligence – everything must be done with care.

By the turn of the 21st century, farming such a compact piece of land was no longer viable. Managing the land had become a second job, as a day job was required to adequately fund outgoings. The community's social and cultural feel was shifting quite dramatically as well. As the sawmilling wound down and the cleared land was used for farming, Lyonville had a stable population of farming families. Many of the descendants of the households listed in the survey of 1886 still live or farm here. And while there is stability on one hand, the inexorable momentum of social change cleaves the fabric of Lyonville. People would complain that the animals smelled or a tractor working at night disturbed them. What was once a productive 30-plus-hectare farm is now four lifestyle blocks earmarked as rural living. Pockets of viable farming still exist in the region, but some of the best soil in Victoria is turned over to large weekenders in striking distance from Melbourne.

When we took over our 9 hectares in 2017, neither Susan nor I had any background in farming. I could certainly grow a few veggies, wield a brush cutter and drive a tractor, but had no agricultural skills to speak of. The property had been a 'lifestyle' hobby farm for a few years and showed the signs of busy people doing their best, but not quite getting there. The fences were shot. The invasive weeds, blackberries, gorse and thistles, were out of control. The buildings were falling down. And the pastures? Damaged by horses' overgrazing. There was much to do.

Purchasing Babbington Park was the beginning of Susan's and my sustainable journey together. We both felt very strongly that we needed to respect this beautiful piece of land and start to remedy some of the ills it had suffered. It would have been lovely to have a good twelve months to sit and ponder which direction to take but, being on the wrong side of fifty, we didn't really have the chance to dawdle. The compromise that we have made is that we do use the ground for the production of food, yet work assiduously to remove invasive weed species and regenerate the waterway at the foot of the hill. It is a balance that works well at the moment, but will grow and change in time, as we learn more about the indigenous trees, plants and grasses, and try to implement more naturalistic plantings.

Our initial priority was getting a vegetable garden up and running as soon as possible. We chose a paddock, which was quite easy, as there are only two flat ones. There is one with a northerly aspect, and the other is more enclosed, so we picked the north-east-facing paddock. Fences, coops and shelter sheds needed to be secured before I could relocate my flocks of birds. Water sources had to be established, for both the garden and poultry. All of these tasks were done with the restraint that is caused by buying something a little out of the budget, but we managed. There is little or no point in looking back and thinking what you would do differently, as that time is gone. Susan and I feel we have mainly made considered decisions and are extremely grateful for my knowledge gained from the Malmsbury garden, so that we have made few of the mistakes I made there. We also bless the small tractor I already owned – this kind of vehicle is a must on a small acreage if things are to get done.

In our first three years, we divided the main three paddocks into six, for better rotational grazing. We removed a number of overgrown cypresses, and other European trees, that were impinging on the landscape. We took loads and loads of things to the tip – mainly concrete that has been used for shoring up on the farm. We found hidden in the long grass piles of asbestos, which needs an expert to remove. The detritus that accumulates while living on a farm is extraordinary, and tidying it is an arduous task, but 'editing' of the property continues unabated. Beautiful things have been discovered, particularly the natural springs. There are seven springs at various points in a line down the western hill. These create a permanent stream that feeds into the lake, a vast body of water. When the lake is full, which it is for about eight months of the year, the overflow meanders down the rest of the hill and feeds into the Loddon. In recent months, we have discovered more springs in a different part of the hill. Our attempts at taming the gorse and blackberries go slowly but are relentless. Again, we are always aware of wanting to leave this place better than when we arrived.

Lyonville itself has retained its village appeal. There are no shops, with a pub being the only commercial endeavour. The community is close, supportive and an absolute delight to live among.

There is a woodcutters' myth that has been handed down through generations of folk. Every so often, the teams of woodcutters would come across a particularly magnificent tree that they could not bring themselves to fell. Those trees are dotted across this region, and we have a manna gum overlooking the house. While she may only be 400 or 500 years old, we know that she grew in a time when the country was starkly different, and she has seen a great deal of slaughter. Of people and of trees. She is yet another constant reminder to tread more lightly; to walk more respectfully.

Recipes inspired by Lyonville's earliest European settlers

This is a collection of recipes inspired by the Cornish settlers in the Lyonville–Bullarto region of Victoria – the site of Babbington Park.

The cream tea

One of the reasons the cream tea is so famous in Cornwall is the amount of land given over to dairy cows. Its damp, green pasture is unsuitable for cropping, but holds well for milk production. Clotted cream is served with Cornish scones, and it is a regional specialty. Cornish soil is not particularly suited to the Rubus fruit family, so the jam of choice was often a plum native to the area. When the settlers came to Victoria, they would not have had the same access to dairy but would have been delighted to be able to grow a greater variety of fruit for jam making and preserving.

Scones

MAKES 12–16
4 cups self-raising flour
¼ cup icing sugar
1 cup cream
1½ cups milk

Preheat the oven to 220°C.

In a large bowl, mix the flour and sugar together.

Pour in the cream and cut into the dry ingredients with a broad-bladed butter knife. This cutting action distributes the cream without over-working the mix.

Add the milk and mix together to form a shaggy mess. Turn onto a lightly floured bench and bring together with light hands. It is important to be gentle with scone dough, so that it doesn't become tough. I always think of it as similar to handwashing my smalls, as opposed to scrubbing my work clothes. Cut into 12–16 squares or rounds, re-forming the offcuts gently to make more. Place on a greased oven tray and bake for 15–20 minutes or until golden brown and cooked through. Remove from the oven and place in a bowl lined with a fresh, clean tea towel. Wrap the scones loosely until you wish to serve.

Basic jam recipe

Homemade jam has become an old friend to me over the years. I work on the following very basic principles: for every kilo of fruit, use a kilo of sugar and the juice of one lemon. It is the maths that I use for all stone fruits, Rubus fruit, strawberries and foraged fruit. When it comes to making sweet jellies, I use 1 litre of strained liquid to 1 kilo of sugar.

This basic approach is not always foolproof. Sometimes my fruit may be a little overripe and won't set so well; sometimes it's a little underripe and sets a little too hard. After all these years, though, I am not terribly fussed by the small inconsistencies of my jam and jelly making. There are plenty of recipes that work better with a softer jam – jellies that are slightly liquid are often great in meat sauces and I'm frequently found rippling ice cream with soft jam.

I do make all my jams in batches no larger than 3 kilos of fruit and use a proper copper wide-mouthed preserving pan. I have found that when you make larger batches than this, it takes too long to come to the setting point and the texture of the fruit deteriorates. In the same vein, using a wide preserving pan enables the quickest evaporation, again making the finished product better. I have found that the other essential piece of equipment is a jam thermometer, either digital or analog. I cook all of my jams and jellies to 104 °C. The reason for this is that jam sets because of the amount of available pectin in the fruit. It doesn't matter how long you keep boiling the jam, it won't set any harder once you exceed this temperature. The only thing you may achieve is creating a slightly acrid flavour from overcooking the sugar.

    1 kg unblemished fruit; a little underripe is better than overripe for
       setting (damaged fruit is best reserved for chutneys and relishes)
    1 kg white sugar
    juice of 1 lemon

If using large fruit, cut into pieces, and remove all pips and stones. Bring the fruit to the boil with the lemon juice.

Add the sugar and stir until dissolved. Boil rapidly, stirring every so often to make sure the jam is not sticking to the bottom of the pan. When the temperature reaches 104 °C, remove from heat and fill sterilised jam jars. Screw on the lids while the jam is still very hot to achieve a vacuum seal.

The Cornish pastie

The Cornish pastie is perhaps Cornwall's most famous culinary export. Few of us stop to think that its popularity in Australia gives us a picture of migration in the 19th century. It is rumoured to have started in the tin mines in Cornwall, when lunch was packed in a – probably inedible – pastry crust. The flat shape of the pastie meant that it could be slipped into a coat pocket and taken out at lunchtime, negating the need to carry lunch boxes into the mine.

My recipe calls on my earliest memories of pasties, which were a very simple affair, and they are cheap and easy to make. I do use a traditional lard or rendered–pork fat pastry. Lard, often seen as the poor man's butter, is widely used in Cornish cookery. It seems a little odd that, with Cornwall's dairy heritage, so much lard was used. Perhaps the traditional Cornish palate wanted cream to be kept for clotting and not given over to the churning of butter.

The lard-pastry recipe can be used for many things other than pasties. I find its plasticity and ease of use make it a delightful casing for little strawberry and rhubarb purse pies when you have a summer abundance of those fruits, and an excellent pastry for cold formed pies, like pork pies or duck pies.

Annie's indestructible lard pastry

200 g lard
200 g plain flour
200 g self-raising flour
a pinch of salt
180 ml water

You can make this pastry on a benchtop by hand, in a bowl by hand, in a stand mixer with the paddle attachment or in a food processor.

Chop the lard into small cubes. Mix the flour and salt, then add the lard and work through until it resembles coarse breadcrumbs.

Make a well, add water, and bring together into a dough. Wrap in cling wrap and chill for 30 minutes. Use as needed.

Traditional pastie

1 potato
1 carrot
1 swede
½ cup frozen peas
1 onion
olive oil
250 g minced beef
1 tbsp chopped parsley
1 tsp Worcestershire sauce
salt and freshly ground pepper
1 quantity lard pastry
1 egg, lightly beaten (i.e. an egg wash)

Peel and chop the three root vegetables into a small dice.

Place in a saucepan of cold water, bring to the boil and simmer until just cooked. Add the peas, cook for a minute or two, then strain and refresh under cold water.

Finely chop the onion. Heat a pan over medium heat, add a splash of oil, add the onion. Cook slowly until soft. Add the mince, turn heat to high and cook, stirring occasionally until the mince is browned. Remove from heat, place in a bowl with vegetables, parsley, Worcestershire, salt and lots of pepper. Mix well.

Preheat oven to 200 °C.

Roll out the pastry and cut into 20-cm circles. Place a good spoonful of filling in each, fold over and seal the edges. Place on a greased tray. Brush with the egg wash and bake for 20 minutes or until golden brown.

Something sweet

A delicious teatime treat found throughout Cornwall, the saffron and currant bun is also known as a revel bun and is favoured by the Methodist Church. The bun was often baked for special occasions associated with the church. Traditionally, those in West Cornwall would bake their buns on a sycamore leaf, leaving a lovely imprint on the bottom. Saffron is the ingredient that distinguishes this bun from the common-or-garden variety that is popular in the rest of Britain. The Romans brought the saffron crocus to England and it has been farmed there, on a small scale, ever since. I am sure that the men who moved to this area from Cornwall nearly 200 years ago would be delighted to know that the towns of Trentham and Glenlyon both boast small-scale saffron farms. Currants also appear in a number of classic Cornish recipes, like the Hevva cake.

Saffron and currant buns

MAKES 12

a large pinch of saffron threads

1 tbsp boiling water

7 g instant yeast (1 sachet)

85 g caster sugar

150 g full cream milk, at blood temperature

600 g bread flour

7 g fine sea salt

125 g unsalted butter

1 egg
100 ml water, at blood temperature
200 g currants

The night before you make the buns, place the saffron in the boiling water and set aside. This helps bring out the maximum flavour and colour from the threads.

Whisk together the dried yeast, sugar, warm milk and warm water. Place the bread flour in a large, wide mixing bowl. Add the salt. Cut the unsalted butter into small cubes, then rub the butter into the flour mixture until well crumbled.

Add the egg and saffron to the milk mixture and then add to the flour mix. Bring together with a spatula until it forms a shaggy dough. Cover with a tea towel and allow to rest for 10 minutes.

Knead the dough until smooth, using a lifting and folding action. Flatten it into a rectangle and scatter the currants over it; knead briefly to combine.

Oil the scraped-out mixing bowl, then return the dough to the bowl, cover with cling wrap or a tea towel and allow to rise until doubled in size (this should take about an hour).

Turn the dough onto a lightly floured surface and gently fold it onto itself. Divide the dough into 12 pieces, then shape each piece into a ball and flatten slightly. Place on a greased baking tray, allowing the pieces room to spread. Preheat the oven to 200°C (with fan).

Allow the buns to prove until doubled in size, in a warm, draught-free place, for about 30 minutes, then bake in the preheated oven for about 15 minutes, until golden brown. Cool on a wire rack and serve with butter or jam or clotted cream, or all three!

The productive garden

THE PRODUCTIVE GARDEN is the cornerstone of our efforts towards sustainability at Babbington Park and du Fermier. It is where we grow as much of the produce for the restaurant and the family as we can. The garden at Malmsbury became what it was with me adding infrastructure as it was needed and as funds were available. At times it was messy, at times it was ad hoc, but these issues were absorbed into the fabric of the property. When I made the move to Lyonville, I was used to a productive garden that had long passed the 'set-up' stage and had settled into being a fully functional entity. When it came to thinking about establishing the new garden, I was whisked away on a cloud of positives, knowing the soil was wonderful and there was an abundance of water. I had forgotten exactly how much infrastructure the old garden had needed over time, but I hoped that, within a season, I would be back to producing vegetables again.

The siting of the vegetable garden and orchard was quite easy. Our piece of land is flattish at the road end and then drifts down a hill to the dam. Given how cold our region is, we needed as much sun as possible, so we selected the paddock on the north side of the property for the productive garden. The area was an easy walk from the house, and reasonably flat, but was terribly vulnerable to wind whipping up the hill from westerly and south-westerly directions. This meant that working out how we wanted the finished plan to look required much thought.

We were on a very tight schedule of getting the Babbington Park garden up and running before we handed over the Malmsbury garden to its new owners. We didn't have the luxury of sitting and watching how the land responded to different seasons and weather patterns. When I planted the first garden at Malmsbury, it was at the tail end of a drought cycle. I learned eighteen months later that I had created my entire vegetable garden on an area that was prone to flooding in wet years. It was a salutary lesson, and, while it is not practical to wait for years until finalising the layout of your garden, I would have preferred to have had at least twelve months.

With the lack of time, we went at it all a little gung-ho, but that is often how you find yourself acting when excited and enthusiastic. That first winter, we cut the initial two blocks, which were approximately 20 square metres. 'Cutting the ground' means removing the sod from the top layer of the paddock to expose the rich earth underneath. We do this with a tractor bucket; in smaller gardens, it is done with a sharp spade. Over the next couple of years, we cut a further six blocks, to make a total of eight. It's a huge area to garden, but at times doesn't seem big enough and at others feels ridiculously too much.

The garden follows different rhythms across the year. From spring through to mid-summer, we are constantly weeding, as the warmth and the water encourage weeds as well as our crops. It is then that you realise you are crawling up and down rows that would cover half a soccer pitch so as to remove all the unwanted occupants. One of the good things about all this weeding is that it is done with a dual purpose. Not only does it clear the beds, allowing all the resources to go to our crops, but we place all the weeds in vats and cover them with water. After stewing it for a few weeks, we decant the contents, use the liquid in our plant-feeding regimens, and can also add the inert drowned weed mush to the compost, where it will never sprout again. We call this our 'weed tea'.

At no stage did we poison the ground before we started, which has meant that in cultivating the earth, we have chopped weed roots through our growing patches. One of the problems of using mechanical aids, such as a rotary hoe, is that it takes any root material and spreads it through your garden beds. In the quest to get the beds prepared as quickly as possible, this is how we prepared the initial rows. It has created a bit of a weed monster for us but, coming up to our fourth growing season, we are hoping we have almost put that problem to bed. If I had had my/our time again, I would have cut the ground, mulched it heavily and put it under cover for a couple of months, to help kill off the weed roots and seeds. We now do this as we go and are very happy with the results. Whenever we have fallow rows, we compost, mulch and cover with tarps to help destroy any weed material.

When we started, I also didn't fully understand the climate. I had no idea of how altitude affects a growing season. It seems that for every 10 metres in height, the ground stays cold for longer. This in turn makes our sowing and growing seasons much shorter than I was used to in Malmsbury.

It also meant that, within a couple of weeks into our first winter, I had to commit to buying a large poly tunnel (much more on this later), as I quickly realised that we needed a good undercover space to extend the growing season. Given that I am supplying both the restaurant and our home, our poly tunnel is 20 by 6 metres. For home gardeners in cold climates, a much smaller one would suffice. In any case, it has proved indispensable, as there is little or no point in grow- ing too many tomatoes, zucchinis, eggplants or cucumbers outside. They are much happier indoors, away from the oddball weather that we often deal with up here on the hill. The poly tunnel was sited so that it also offered the vegetable garden protection from the winds whistling up from the south west.

Over the next couple of years, we planted a hedge of hundreds of hazelnut bushes to grow up around the vegetable garden, to create a buffer to the outside and a microclimate on the inside. The wind protection for the vegetable garden has been further boosted by the siting and planting of the orchard on the western side of the vegetable area. The trees selected are all grafted onto full-size rootstock, which means they will be tall specimen trees. This will not only create a beautiful shaded canopy but will help with the buffering of the western winds. The orchard has been hedged with a classic English-style selection of plants. We will allow this to grow to 2 metres tall, which will protect the fruit trees when they are young and turn into a magnificent statement of its own as it becomes twisted, tangled and impenetrable as the years go by.

Our time here in Lyonville has made me embrace the seasons from a different perspective. With European colonisation came European seasons – but the structure of spring, summer, autumn and winter is woefully inadequate to describe the shifts in our weather. The Indigenous peoples of the area have a much more nuanced approach to describing the seasons: in the Gariwerd region, just west of Lyonville, the Jardwadjali and Djab Wurrung people recognise six weather periods. These distinctions are much more apt for the area than the blanket European seasonal structure. The Gariwerd seasons give me further insight into what to expect from the climate here, and show me just how much we have to learn from the First Peoples.

However, as we cycle through the seasons over the years, it is becoming more and more obvious that the local conditions are changing dramatically. The growing of plants for food and decoration follows some basic principles. Day length is one of the most impor-tant. The internal clocks of seeds and plants are very aware of the daylight hours available to them. This does not change; what does change are the climatic conditions that evolve during those days. Seasonal fluctuations have always been a part of food production;

weather patterns come and go, much like a boom-and-bust cycle. In some ways, they used to be much easier to predict, but the ravages of climate change alter these patterns and intensify the effects. Wind and heat are seemingly on the rise. What this means, on a very basic and practical level for me, is that I need to be constantly aware of the needs of each plant. I plant seasonally according to the European calendar I know best, I refer to the Indigenous weather periods for deeper understanding, but I concentrate on tailoring care of each plant to that particular day and its conditions.

We have made many mistakes in setting up the garden here at Lyonville. To me, though, mistakes are not always a problem. In cooking, I always find that I learn a great deal from dishes I have made or recipes I have created that have not worked out so well. I find they make me think about, and come to understand, the processes at hand better than does a straight-up success. In gardening, as in cooking, there are so many approaches you can take, the odds are that you will make a misstep here and there, including doing something that doesn't quite work for your piece of land. There is never a day that we are not up for another crazy science experiment in the garden. Many of them succeed, but we can always have a bit of a giggle at those that are massive failures. That is unless, of course, they were expensive, in which case laughter would not be seemly!

I am intensely proud of what we have achieved in the garden over these last years, and have had the most amazing support and input from some really special and talented people. James and Kieran work with me on our plot, and are generous, gifted, wonderful men. The interchange of knowledge and ideas at the start of our days is something I always look forward to. Usually, we have our walk around and, after the tasks for the day are decided, I head to the work kitchen, usually with an 'I've got to go, I'm late.' I will come back to the garden after they have gone and do my tasks, and I always feel a pull: I want to be in the garden as much as I want to be in the kitchen.

The vegetable, fruit and flower gardens

The eight blocks that we refer to as 'The Vegetable Garden' combine fruit growing, vegetable growing and flower growing. The four blocks on the northern side are dedicated to perennial plants. We have done this so that the perennial side will grow into another layer of wind protection for the more delicate annual crops.

Block 2

This houses our rhubarb and some of our berry fruit. The whole block is netted to maximise our fruit production. In the first row (we number from the western to eastern edge for each block) is the rhubarb. All of these plants were lifted from Malmsbury and divided. Every three years, we pull them up, divide them again, remulch and compost the bed and return the smaller crowns to the ground. The rest we pot up and give to any takers. The variety is a good red version that is great for baking and stewing. Rhubarb is incredibly hungry, so it needs to be fed to produce strong yields. We feed it a lot of our weed tea, particularly through the summer months.

Next to the rhubarb are four rows of raspberries. The first two rows are of the Heritage variety. This is a cultivar that has become very popular with the home gardener, as it is easier to look after than some others. The canes all get cut to the ground at the end of each season. These bear fruit during autumn, and if the start of winter is mild, can still be producing fruit in the first few weeks of June. The second two rows are full of a variety called Chilcotin.

This is a summer fruiting variety that grows its fruit on *last* year's canes. This means selective pruning each winter to separate out the spent canes from the productive canes. We prune them so that each year we start with about ten canes per plant, which is the optimal number for productivity.

All these plants came from a small block of raspberries that were on the farm near the old glasshouse site when we arrived. They have been identified and divided, and form the 80 metres of canes we now care for. Raspberries are prolific growers and send up many suckers, which need to be pulled out; and we expend a great deal of time and love on them, making sure that there are not too many, and that they are fed and kept weed free. At the beginning of their dormant period, the canes are thinned out dramatically. We trim them and package them up as bare-rooted plants for others to have in their own gardens.

The raspberries are grown using a traditional structure of wood and wire to keep them supported. The end posts are set into the ground with three pieces of wood, about 50 centimetres in length, nailed across the posts lengthways at three levels. Wire is attached to each end of these and strung the length of the bed. We have also constructed metre-wide paths between each row. This is necessary as, come full summer and autumn, when their growth is prodigious, even with a metre-wide path the tunnel of green growth can become almost impenetrable.

We pick raspberries from December through to late May. It is a labour of love, takes forever and requires a systematic approach. I will never forget one early morning when I was picking the raspberries with James and he commented that it reminded him of when the nit nurse came to school! I see where he is coming from, as you just methodically work through each cane to find the fruit. Many's the podcast I have listened to while picking berries. At least the raspberries are a standing-up picking job, which is a welcome relief for our backs after a season of picking other berries either at ground level or while kneeling.

Next to the raspberries are the rest of the Rubus fruit. I have selected four different cultivars: silvanberries, loganberries, thornless blackberries and boysenberries. All these varieties produce fruit from last year's canes, so we prune them in a similar way to, but with a slightly different set-up from, how we prune the Chilcotin raspberries. The brambles are all trained on single wires. Between each end post are strung five wires about 30 centimetres apart, so that we can train the berries at different heights. The fruiting of all these start with the silvans and the logans; it is after the strawberries, but before the raspberries, in early summer. The blackberries ripen

in late summer. The boysenberries do a bit of both. The silvanberries and blackberries are prolific performers; we get kilos and kilos and kilos of fruit. The silvans are a horror to pick, as the canes are very prickly. By the time I am up to the stage of picking the blackberries, I am well and truly over thorns. The logans and boysens are no more friendly than the silvans, but they produce less fruit, so I spend less time being prickled by them.

As we move through the seasons with these four cultivars, there is a series of steps and manoeuvres we make. We start with a path that is a metre wide. While these do not tunnel like the raspberries, as they are trained laterally, we need a great deal of safe space to encourage the new growth that will be next year's crop. At the beginning of the growing season, we have all of last year's canes tied to the wires. As the spring growth arrives, these tied canes become abundant with new life, and get bigger and longer; this is where the flowering and the fruit set happens. As the season goes on, the new canes start to emerge from the base of the plants. These we allow to grow laterally along the ground on the paths. This is so that when it comes to selecting them and tying them up for the next season, we have a clear division of old and new. It is clear by the colour of the stalk, but there is so much business with old growth, new growth, flowers and fruit that we find it easier this way. Again, though, it does mean that harvesting the berries is like kneeling amid Medusa's snakes, and there is definitely a place for sturdy thorn-proof trousers. After all the work is done for the season and the cold has arrived, we work through all the canes, removing the old ones, untying the canes from the wires, selecting those that will be kept for the following year and tying them to the wires – a perfect representation of life through the seasons.

Next to the rows of Rubus fruit are two of strawberries. These are the original plants that were lifted from the Malmsbury garden. There are two varieties: an unknown large cultivar, and a small, soft, sweet berry, the Cambridge Rival.

We only keep our strawberries in the ground for three seasons, collecting runners each year and starting subsequent rows; and then lifting the original plants, feeding, mulching and resting the beds for a year before we start the process again. We are vigilant at picking off runners during the fruiting season, so that we get as much fruit as possible and the plants are not distracted by fuelling leaf growth. The strawberries are the earliest to fruit, in mid-spring. They continue until the silvanberries start. Once they have slowed or stopped fruiting, we give them a very drastic prune, clipping them right back. The plants then start the cycle again and we get a small, but delicious, crop of the larger strawberry in autumn. It is worth noting that the spring fruit and the late summer and autumn fruit taste completely different. They tell a story about the day's length and the sun's strength just by their flavour difference.

Block 4

This is the second of our dedicated fruit blocks. Here, we house our Ribes fruit: blackcurrants, redcurrants and whitecurrants, and gooseberries. Like the berries, these are all plants that will see us through many years, with good luck and care. The Ribes fruit are also gross feeders, loving being mulched with our manure-rich compost. It is when we start using all the mulch made from our animal bedding that I understand the complex nature of successfully creating a sustainable life. It is the circular nature of all we do that creates the entire fabric of the place. While we don't eat any of the birds or animals, the keeping of them allows us the joys of companionship, ensures that the pastures are mown and gives us manure-soaked bedding that, in turn, feeds our hungry plants.

Like many of the berries, the currants mainly grow their fruit on one-year canes. Unlike with the berries, though, we don't prune all the old canes out each year. We encourage the plant to grow into a robust, upstanding specimen, and give careful attention to making sure that the middle of the plant isn't too crowded, so there is space and air available for the flowers and fruit when they come. At least, that's the goal with the blackcurrants, but the whites and the reds have a different growing habit and tend to flop about a great deal more, making them the difficult children of the family. If they get too unruly, we drive a stake in and wrap an old stocking, or something similar, around the currants to keep them contained. We purchased the redcurrants and whitecurrants as stock, but the blackcurrants are another reminder of the Malmsbury garden. Before we left, we took fifty-odd cuttings, and struck them here at Babbington Park. They flourished and, each year, I still give away cuttings so that others can enjoy the plants, as well as the fruit in the restaurant.

The gooseberries are few and a folly. I really planted them so that, at some point in my life, I could make gooseberry fool from my own fruit. I am sure that I will use them in jams or desserts when they flourish and fruit, but as they are young plants, I may need to wait a couple of years for that.

The balance of the block is reserved for our plan of continuous strawberry propagation. At present, there are another three rows of two- and one-year-old strawberry plants, with more coming this season. The rows that have been waiting for their strawberries have been put to good use over the last three years. This is where I have been planting out my stock of nursery plants that I've been propagating from seed and cuttings, and dividing from the decorative garden. As the garden beds around the house are designed and filled, it is wonderful knowing that we are buying as few plants as possible and growing most of the stock from seed.

Block 6

This block houses a series of very long-term vegetable crops. It is the home of the artichokes, the asparagus and the hard herbs. Rosemary, a shrub that grows all year round, is the first of these. Oregano and marjoram grow most of the year but are cut back in winter. The same goes for our cooking sage and thyme varieties. Lovage, a curious herb that tastes like celery, is quite frost tender and dies back after the first frosts, only to be renewed in late spring.

The artichokes start the block – a little like the rhubarb. Their similarities don't stop there. The artichokes are a long-term crop that will be there for years. Every three to five years, we will get in there and divide the plants, so that their productive nature is kept up. It is a bit of a mystery to me as to why I continue to grow these, as they are not my favourite vegetable, partly due to the amount of effort needed to prepare them as against the net end result. However, the foliage's structure and colour, a strong silvery green, add to the garden in many ways. I am also fascinated by their growth habitat. When the artichokes appear, they are similar to heading broccoli. The first to appear is the large central 'nonna'. Then come a few 'mammas' around the outside and, further into the season, a proliferation of 'bambini'. On a cooking level, this gives me one showily large artichoke to present as a course in the restaurant. Then the mammas and the bambini can all be used for collective dishes, like salads, pastas and pizzas.

The asparagus is one of my favourite crops in the garden. In the first three of seven rows, we have a variety called Mary Washington. She is the standard thin-style asparagus. Buying them as crowns from a proper breeder, we ensure that there will only be male plants. This maximises the strength of the spears and means we don't have the berries falling in the autumn from female plants. The berries love to take root and become new plants, but we can't afford to overcrowd these beds. The asparagus being another energetic feeder – gosh, I've got a hungry garden – we need to maintain a strict number of plants per row, as they will, hopefully, live there for another twenty-five years.

Asparagus is a waiting game. First, it is best not to pick it for the first couple of years. This will ensure that the plant puts all of its energy into its own growing cycle, which strengthens the crown for the future – a bit like laying solid foundations for a building. After being patient for the first couple of years, you should then confine yourself to only harvesting spears for about six weeks. Again, this preserves the crown and helps keep it going productively for its long and generous life span. Don't ever forget that each year the crown gets bigger and bigger, and you are rewarded with more and more.

After the Mary Washington, we have the dividing row of hard herbs: several thymes, oregano, cooking sage, tarragon, rosemary and a little lovage.

Then come four rows of Argenteuil, an asparagus cultivar that we have grown from seed. I have very high hopes for this plant. It is an old French heirloom variety that is not only robust enough to pick a little of in its second year, but is *the* asparagus to blanch. My dream is that Mary will provide all our standard green asparagus, and I will be able to keep all my Argenteuil bundled up in layers of straw to grow into the thick white spears that adorn the markets in France in early spring.

There are still a few rows vacant in block 6. I have toyed with the idea of growing Tuscan kale there as a permanent crop rather than treating it as an annual, as I like the symmetry of two Italian vegetables framing each end of the bed. However, if our asparagus thrives, there is another heirloom variety I would like to plant: Connover's Colossal. That, though, is a decision for the future.

Block 8

This is the prettiest of all the blocks. I feel that no productive garden would be complete without a flower-cutting garden. While most of this block is planted out with herbaceous peonies, it is also the area where I grow rows of poppies, larkspurs, delphiniums, scabiosa, cornflowers and nigella. Not only does growing flowers help prodigiously with our pollination rates, it provides the restaurant with beautiful blooms for months. Like the asparagus and the artichokes, the peonies will last for decades. I often wonder quietly if some of these very long-term ones will become a lovely little cash crop for my dotage. I imagine eighty-year-old Annie out there – muttering away to the plants, tending them, loving them, and expecting them to be like all good children: prepared to look after their mother when she is old.

Blocks 1, 3, 5 and 7

While there is order, discipline and longevity in the northern blocks, the same cannot be said for the southern blocks used for annual and rotating crops. While we try to minimise the sense of chaos, the cycle of rotational growing brings its own messy look to all these blocks. There are plants that are just about to be pulled out, others that are just emerging, and some that are in their full flight, which all creates a slight sense of unruliness. Across the seasons and across the rotations, it feels like there are hundreds of different plants and varieties coming and going from our lives.

We plant in a cyclical way, calling on the biodynamic moon calendar for directions on what to plant when: leafy greens one week, fruiting and flowering crops the next, and root vegetables in the third week.

As the years have passed, we are almost at the stage where we can discipline ourselves to use one block for predominantly the same style of vegetable. Often the desire to break the rules and slip something else in, just because there is a modicum of space, wins and careful symmetry goes out the window, but we do try.

Recently, we changed our sowing methods quite dramatically. We had done a great deal of direct sowing into the garden, but we are moving towards a much more disciplined approach and using the multi-sown seedling method more and more. Multi-sowing is when we sow our seed in trays in individual modules, with some three to five seeds per module, depending on the variety. The plant develops in a controlled environment where both the roots and the stems are stronger. This allows for much better survival rates and placement when being transplanted into the garden.

Across the four blocks, we try to have at least the equivalent of one under a green manure crop, or 'solarised'. Solarisation is where we compost heavily and cover it with tarpaulin to kill off any emerging weed stock. We always strive to have that amount of ground fallow, so that the soil can rest and regenerate. As mentioned, we do grow green manure crops, which are ploughed back into the ground; and tillage crops, which break up the soil and are then ploughed back in. The green manure crop is a mixture of seeds that will grow into nitrogen-fixing plants, and the tillage crop is a daikon crop that grows radishes about 45 centimetres deep. This helps to break up the soil underneath the rows, and allow better root and nutrient penetration for the plants that follow.

Across the seasons, we grow a wide variety of plants. As the climate is cold, we don't plant outside any earlier than September and don't tend to plant anything after March. The cycles of the soil heating and cooling directly affect germination and plant growth, so we limit ourselves to these months for the best results. Needless to say, most places are much warmer than Lyonville and therefore have much longer sowing and planting windows.

Our choice of plants is based on what I know I will use in both the restaurant and at home. We grow a broad selection of cut-and-come-again salad crops, as well as heading lettuces. There is spinach: both English and a perennial variety that is closer to silverbeet than spinach. There is rainbow chard, lamb's lettuce, radicchio and celtuce in the less mainstream crops; broccolis, cauliflowers in four different colours, brussels sprouts, cabbage variations; beans – climbing, bush and broad; peas, snow peas and snap peas; tomatoes, zucchinis, peppers and eggplants; cucumbers, and pickling cucumbers and melons; radishes, carrots, beetroots, turnips, swedes and mangelwurzels; garlic, onions, shallots, leeks and spring onions. I am quite sure that this is not a complete list, but it serves to illustrate the extensive variety of crops that we grow and manage from small seeds to productive plants.

I can never stress strongly enough that this largesse does not translate sensibly to the home garden. Too much of multiple vegetables, and eating the same thing over again, can sometimes dampen the spirits, unlike the joy of producing just enough and having a variation of crops. There are practical ways to work out how to do this. First, try to grow from seed or buy your seedlings singly – or be prepared to give some of the punnet away. Consult a vegetable yield chart! The sort of information I glean from one of these charts is this: for a 30-metre row, you would fit fifty broccoli plants. The yield of these would be approximately 40 kilograms; the recommended planting per person is three to five plants. With carrots, the recommended sowing amount per person is 1.5 to 3 metres. This gives you the opportunity to calculate just how much space you need to dedicate to each vegetable you want to grow, and helps you with rotational planting. Sometimes I sit and dream of a Mr McGregor-style vegetable garden worked out as precisely as this; I imagine I could spend hours working on the minutiae of it.

The poly tunnel

In cold climates such as ours, the poly tunnel is an invaluable piece of growing space. It extends our growing season and allows us to grow crops with significant yields that would struggle to produce in the outside environment. Again, the poly tunnel is some 20 by 6 metres. Its size means that it does not hold the heat terribly successfully through winter, but it does protect plants from direct crop damage. So, we also have a small and inexpensive plastic house that we use as our propagation area. It is equipped with a couple of tube heaters and a couple of heat mats, to encourage seed germination in July, August and September. In time, I hope to graduate to a more permanent structure of a small glasshouse to raise seeds in the winter.

Our work patterns follow the seasons. From late July, we start sowing seeds in our little propagation house, in small cell trays or small soil blocks. Once the plant has enough root mass to hold the amount of soil it is planted in, it is transplanted into a bigger pot. We might change the pot size three times before something is planted out into the soil. This is usually because the weather conditions are not yet quite favourable enough to plant out, and the sprout needs the space and soil to continue to thrive. Once the seedling has graduated from its small tray to a small pot, it is transferred from the prop house to the poly tunnel. As we have begun growing most of our beetroots, turnips and parsnips by the multi-sown method, we start these seeds in slightly larger cell trays. This is so that more root development is possible before planting out, as we find these varieties only really like one transplant.

The poly tunnel starts getting prepared in mid-September for the bounty of crops we associate with summer and autumn. It houses our zucchinis, eggplants, peppers, cucumbers, melons, early beans and broccoli and basil.

At the beginning of each season, I allocate the plants, which will be in there for many months, to the six beds. This gives us a chance to prepare the soil and all the hanging apparatus we use for our tomatoes and cucumbers. We grow both these plants up vertical pieces of string, trimming a lot of the leaf as they grow, to allow the fruit the most amount of light and air as it grows. It always amazes me that this configuration of plants fills the poly tunnel for eight months of the year. In the 'off' season, we use the space for lettuces and salad greens, beetroot and the perennial plants that I am growing from seed.

At one end of the poly tunnel, we attach pieces of house guttering to the timber framework. These are used for the early strawberries.

In late winter, we fill them with soil and add small strawberry plants. These blossom in the early spring warmth inside the poly tunnel and give us a small, but delicious, early crop of strawberries before the main crop starts. At the other end of the poly tunnel, we have racks and tables to hold all our seedlings in their various states of development.

The poly tunnel is a very busy hub of our world, and a complete necessity in the local climate. A word of advice about them, though: if the climate you're in requires something like this for your sufficiency needs, I would suggest always purchasing a tunnel that has roll-up sides. While they are a more expensive option, if you don't have one when summer hits, you could fry all your plants, or use a ridiculous amount of water trying to cool them off.

The compost area

Every productive garden needs a compost area. Its dual purpose is to consume all the garden and kitchen waste and, after time, gift you beautiful nutrient-rich soil to return to the garden. Ours is vast. It's vast because we have an enormous amount of animal bedding to deal with, endless weeds, and large amounts of leaf tops and trimmings from the crops that we grow.

Compost areas can be strangely visually delightful. However, ours are not neat wooden bays with compost in various states of decay – they are just large heaps of material in neat rows. We compost like this because we have the luxury of a small tractor to turn and form these heaps, a much easier proposition than hand turning with a shovel. We use the classic principles of layering green waste with hay and manure, a little lime and water.

Among our rows, we also have a pile known as 'The Dirty Compost'. This is where all our nasty weeds go if our weed-tea barrels are full. The invasive weeds that we deal with, sorrel, clover and a mix of other unpleasant flat weeds, need to be stored away from the dirt we will use on the garden beds in our day-to-day activities. Once composted down, we use this dirt around the main garden in areas where we need to control weed growth, if we haven't managed to kill it all in the composting process.

The orchard

My planning of fruit tree varieties, and their use, at Babbington was based purely on my successes and failures at Malmsbury. Growing for a restaurant is a very different planning exercise than designing and planting a domestic orchard. On a domestic scale, it is important to grow a variety of trees that produce an array of fruit through the seasons, with some that needs to be eaten immediately and some that can be stored. The restaurant works on slightly different parameters. I need to plant a number of the same trees so that I can feature a range of fruit across a whole weekend; this means having multiples of any one variety is important. And in the restaurant, I am trying to cook as seasonally as possible, so storing fruit is not as important as it is in the domestic environment.

For the Malmsbury garden, I had chosen many apple trees based solely on their names: Catshead, Peasgood Nonsuch and the like. When perusing fruit tree catalogues, I often get distracted from the fruits' purpose by the wonderful names, and can't help ordering some of the special ones. With heritage apples, each apple has a particular cooking structure. Some turn to fluff when subjected to heat; some hold their shape and absorb the flavours of caramel or butter. Each has its specific place in the kitchen.

The orchard at Malmsbury contained about forty trees. There were apples, pears, quinces, crabapples, figs, almonds, plums; all grafted onto dwarf rootstock, which is very popular with a lot of the heritage orchardists, and guarantees a tree that will be of a manageable size for pruning and netting. Once the trees had come to fruit-bearing age, after about three years, I was inundated with fruit – hundreds and hundreds of kilos.

I had multiple crabapple trees of different varieties. The crab-apples were great dual-purpose trees: they had beautiful blossom in spring and, in autumn, were heavy bearers of pretty fruit that is great for making jelly. They were prolific, producing sacks upon sacks of crabapples each autumn. By the end of my life at Malmsbury, there was never enough time to process all the fruit and some of the crabs were turned into compost.

The quinces were as industrious as the crabs; our tree of Champion quinces was a champion by name and champion by nature, providing well over 200 quinces a season. The tree's European cousins, de Vanja and Bourgeot, planted a couple of years later, were well on the way to keeping up with Champion's production when we left. Pears, by nature, were slower, but the apples were overwhelming.

Some of my Heritage apples were good for storing, but I found the sheer volume of them difficult to manage in racks and sheds that were not built for this purpose. I would often gaze at English designer Jasper Conran's pictures of storage sheds in old English apple orchards and wish they were mine. A proper fruit storage shed would have purpose-built wooden racks lining the walls, for the fruit to be placed on without touching each other. This is an echo of a past when cold storage fruit wasn't used.

My point is that the excitement of reading the catalogue and ordering this and that can turn into an abundance of fruit that can be difficult to deal with in any environment other than a commercial orchard. While it is enormously rewarding to succeed so well, there is also something saddening about not being able to use or give away all the fruit. And even more distressing is when you don't have the appropriate storage and bad fruit spoils good fruit. As a result of these lessons from my embarrassment of riches at Malmsbury, my decision-making when planning the orchard at Babbington Park was much better informed.

The initial orchard trees were planted in our second winter. Again, they were chosen based on the knowledge that I had gleaned from Malmsbury and my awareness of what would best suit the restaurant over the coming years. Each variety was chosen for its specific role. The first – and I think the most important – was Calville Blanc d'Hiver. As I talked about earlier, this is a French apple whose sole purpose in life is to make a perfect tarte Tatin. (Doyenné du Comice and D'Anjou pears came in a close second for puff-pastry tarts.) We also planted Morello cherries, D'Agen plum/prune trees, and a couple of peach trees.

Once more, all the stock was on dwarf rootstock. It was decided that the most efficient way of dealing with these trees was to espalier them between the vegetable garden blocks. This made sense on many levels. When I was in Malmsbury, I had issues with some of my apples being too big for the tree they were on. This might sound a little odd, but a series of 900-gram Catshead apples on a branch coming from dwarf rootstock can pull the tree down and set it at an angle. Knowing that the winds were fierce, it was important that the espalier wires would give the tree an enormous amount of support on a root and branch level; too, they gave an air of design to the blocks of vegetables. Second, the espaliering of fruit makes pruning, picking and caring for it much easier and more time efficient. Last, and possibly most importantly, the runs of espaliers are much easier to net than the traditional vase-shaped tree. The simple star picket and poly pipe set-up, on a narrow scale, that we use on the berry and currant cages works fabulously to protect the fruit from the birds and is easy to access. (Poly pipe is the generic name given to the black plastic irrigation pipe that is found on most farms. It comes in various diameters and has many uses other than for irrigation.) This method of growing fruit trees is also the most efficient one in urban areas. On walls facing north, or within smaller gardens, the espaliering method allows many small-plot gardeners to grow an enormous amount of fruit in confined spaces.

The main orchard came into being a year later, an exercise that was defined by my love of plants and trees. In a sense, I have more than enough fruit-producing plants in the main vegetable garden to see me through, but the romantic in me desperately wanted what I refer to as 'The Orchard'.

This area is adjacent to the poly tunnel and houses, among other things, our enormous compost-heap system. It is also the site of the

pigeonnier (of which, more later) and the 10-metre-long stainless-steel duck pond. Once the house is renovated, it will also be our view to the north from our kitchen windows.

The orchard is full of trees that have been grafted onto full-size rootstock. This means there will be an abundance of large-scale fruit trees in twenty years, trees that can never really be netted and are grown for the sheer enjoyment of what magnificent specimens they are. I can almost see them now. I am sure the birds will leave us some fruit, but the geese and the ducks will have their fill of windfall fruit across the late summer and autumn.

There is also a greater variety of trees in the orchard than in the controlled area: quinces; pomegranates; mulberries, both white and purple; sweet cherries; medlars; almond and a couple of walnut trees. It is as if having an orchard full of big trees and a bounty of fruit will mean I realise one of my romantic notions about living in the country.

The whole area is surrounded by a carefully curated English hedgerow. This is full of hawthorns, field maples, sloes, honeysuckles, rugosa roses and filberts. The combination of these plants will create a thicket that is a pleasure dome for insects and small birds, with multiple sweet sickly nectars and fruits for them to sup on. On a design level, the hedgerow will serve as a windbreak for the orchard and start to create a microclimate, like the hazelnuts do in the vegetable garden. When the trees are established, they, in turn, will protect the vegetable garden from the wicked winds that run up the hill. The result is that, while it is all very beautiful, it also makes a great deal of sense for the production levels of our vegetable crops.

We bought quite a number of the trees for the orchard, but many others came from us espaliering the first trees in the vegetable garden. Back when we purchased our first trees, we also bought full-size rootstock, so that the pieces we pruned from the plants to be espaliered could be grafted onto the purchased rootstock. Those plants were then potted up, fed and watered through the year, and then planted out in the orchard during the third winter. This meant that we not only saved a little money but got double the value out of our initial trees.

Core principles and instruction manuals

The winter is when I dedicate the most time to planning the vegetable garden for the coming season. Our soil becomes very cold, and most things in the vegetable garden are either dormant or very slow. This gives me ample time to study the various charts and books that I work from when I plan the coming months. I allocate which plants will go there, and determine how many of each we will need and a sowing regimen for the next six months.

There are a number of references I consult. First is a comprehensive sowing chart. Most seed retailers have one in the gardening-information section on their websites. I use the one from Dandenongs-based supplier The Seed Collection. It gives you all the information you need about sowing across the various climate regions of Australia: sowing depth, row and plant spacings, whether a plant is frost hardy, sowing direct or raising seedlings, germination times and time to maturity. If, for example, you are worried about why the parsnip seeds haven't come up yet, a quick check will reveal that the sprouts can take up to thirty days to appear. What the chart doesn't tell you is temperatures for germination. Many vegetables have different temperatures that they will germinate at, so I have a little print-out of the planting guide that is hand-annotated with the temperatures for various seeds. Tomatoes like it warm, lettuce likes it a little cooler, and radishes are good sports and will germinate almost all year round.

The next thing I consult is a companion planting chart. As we try to maximise our use of row space in the garden, it allows me to check suitability of crops for time sharing. A good example is that I can plant a row of radishes when I plant out my heading lettuce seedlings; the radishes will be harvested before the lettuces' growth interferes with them. Lettuce goes well with the slow-growing parsnip too. It is also prudent to check a chart that shows you what *not* to plant together, so that time isn't wasted; for example, beans love carrots but detest leeks and peppers. The companion planting principles help not only with space use but have the very beneficial effect of deterring insects and pests. You might want to plant some oregano near your brassica plants, as it is one way to deter the cabbage moth.

Then comes the biodynamic planting guide. This is one of the absolute pillars in our yearly organisation. While we do not follow all the principles of biodynamic gardening, we find the planting guide exerts a wonderful discipline in our busy lives, as it gives us knowledge about the pattern of sowing, which aligns with the phases of the moon. So, one week, we sow leafy greens; the next week, we are sowing fruiting vegetables; and the third week, root vegetables. The fourth week is a 'grey' one, for weeding, composting, mowing and catching up with tasks that have gotten away from us (usually weeding). Not only does this discipline keep us on top of our sowing, it helps us later in the cycle to remember where things were planted, so that we can rotate beds and blocks through the leaf/fruit/root cycle.

Then there is the combination that I use of old and new technology. There are several English-garden Instagram accounts that I follow assiduously. One is @daylesfordfarm, which has some excellent Instagram TV pieces on tomatoes, cucumbers and sweet peas, and on how to sow, how to transplant, and how to trellis and keep productive. Another inspirational English account is @charles_dowding. He is one of the greatest exponents of no-dig gardening, and teaches not only how to garden with minimal digging but is a great source of information on trellising and training various plants. We live in an era when there is an enormous amount of material on the internet, and most questions can be answered; it's just a matter of finding who knows about your style and type of garden, and/or is your type of person.

In terms of the old technology, I have three favourite books I refer to. The first is very old: a slim volume first published in 1838, called *Manual of Practical Gardening, adapted to the climate of Van Diemen's Land*. It is a month-by-month guide to the management of the kitchen, of fruit, the flower garden, nursery, greenhouse and forcing departments, where there are allocated areas for placing cloches over rhubarb, cucumbers and asparagus to change the colour, flavour and speed of production of these varieties. The content is written in an old-fashioned style but is very clear and precise.

The second book was a gift from some friends: the fifth edition of *The Weekly Times Farmers' Handbook*, which was published around 1950. It has a great deal of excellent advice and practical techniques, but there is a great deal that is not so useful; the number of times that DDT is mentioned in the management of vegetables and fruit trees is staggering. But the book is also a font of knowledge when it comes to basic animal husbandry and farming techniques.

The third book is the *Reader's Digest Illustrated Guide to Gardening*. This is a complete anthology of care and maintenance of all manner of plants, from identification to espalier techniques. I can curl up in bed with my trusty *Reader's Digest* the night before a specific task is scheduled and learn all about how to approach it.

Planting methods

With all the many varieties of plants that we grow, we have numerous planting methods. These also change with the seasons, as warmer weather and soil can alter the way that many things germinate and grow, affecting how we sow the same seed across a series of sequential plantings.

Following our moon planting guide allows us to easily monitor the progress of monthly sequential plantings. I often marvel that, for example, a broccoli seedling sown in September can end up at exactly the same point as a broccoli seed sown in November, simply because the air and soil temperature are higher and the day length is longer.

Our leafy greens are sown in a number of ways. Heading lettuces are grown from individual seeds, as single plants, and planted in neat rows once the seedling has established good roots and a number of leaves. We start these in small cells and then transplant them into the garden.

Rocket, mizuna, mibuna and other smaller-leafed varieties are multi-sown in cell trays. This gives us three or four plants per cell that are planted out in neat rows. We have turned to this method because we find it makes it much easier to pick the crop, and to avoid cutting any weed material that may have grown up between each plant. When we have direct sown in lines, we have had trouble with grass and weeds featuring in our lettuce mix. Having said that, when we thin out root crops like leeks and beetroots, we form a channel down the middle of these rows and sow cut-and-come-again lettuce mixes. These are lettuces that we don't allow to head, and cut as a lettuce mix–style salad. After forming a clean channel between the root crop with a square-bladed hoe, we mix a small amount of lettuce seed in a barrow of clean and weed-free compost and backfill the channel, being vigilant in spotting any stray weed growth while the seeds are germinating.

Our cress mixes – tatsoi, kale, mustard cress, baby rocket – we do sow directly in rows. The seed is mixed with quite a bit of sand to thin out the plants, because if the seed-to-sand ratio is too high, the plants struggle to thrive. It also enables us to see the rows in the dark soil. These rows are then covered by a thin layer of compost. We have yet to perfect our timing, but we do try to flame weed this crop before it germinates. This is the process of running a flame torch over the ground after any weeds have germinated but before the cress mix germinates. We sow these varieties straight into the ground because we cut them as a very small leaf for garnishing purposes, much like the hydroponic micro-herb pots you can buy commercially.

With the bigger plants in the fruiting varieties, there are some that we direct sow and some that grow through the more laborious route of the propagation house and transplanting. Tomatoes are sown in small cells and then transplanted twice before planting out. Zucchinis, eggplants, peppers and cucumbers are all sown in small cells and transplanted into bigger pots once before planting out. Beans, broad beans and peas, we direct sow. Garlic is direct sown; onions and shallots are grown in seed punnets and then transplanted. Leeks get a mixture of both. The Brassica family is all sown in cell trays, and then transplanted into a bigger container and placed into the ground.

Root vegetables are grown in several different ways. Carrots are mixed with sand and then direct sown in rows. With beetroot, turnips, parsnips and swedes, we now almost exclusively use the multi-sown cell technique, for good yields, and better planting practices that help us with our weed control.

All this being said, if you are a home gardener who doesn't want to muck about with seed raising, you would be buying your seedlings ready to plant. Make sure that the punnet or container is well watered before you turn it out. Dig over the ground that you are going to be planting into, so that you have friable earth and a good fine tilth. Make sure there is a good amount of organic matter, so

that the developing roots can breathe as the plant grows and prospers. Water the plant in once it has been planted. Be sensitive to each plant's needs, especially as to seasonal variations. Does it need mulching to protect it from hot or cold? Will you need to stake the plant in the future and would it be easier to do that at planting? Do you need to make immediate provision for protecting it from pests?

There is nothing sadder than planting out fresh new seedlings and putting off laying pest deterrent until the next day, only to find everything was eaten overnight.

And I cannot stress enough: *don't overplant*. Consult all the manuals and plant accordingly. The results when you do this will always be superior.

When we plant bigger plants that need holes, I always remember a lesson I learned years ago from a gardener working at Malmsbury: dig a square hole – get the spade and dig four sides. The explanation was that corners encourage the plant to grow out, while a round hole encourages the plant to grow roots around and around, sometimes resulting it in being 'potbound', even though it is planted out in the ground. We are incredibly fortunate with the ground that we have here – it is quite easy to dig holes in – but my years at Malmsbury taught me that it can be a very arduous experience. We dig oversize holes and backfill with compost, to make sure there is some lovely soft soil for the plant to nestle in.

Don't forget that the whole process of being transplanted is incredibly traumatic for any plant, no matter its size. The shock of being taken from one environment to another, where the soil is different, and temperature of both air and soil is different, can sometimes be too much for a plant. It is important to take every step to try to make that transition as smooth as possible. Being aware of the issue is the first and most important part.

One of the great joys of raising food from seed is that I have known the plant since its inception. There is a quiet bond with, and enormous pride in, everything that ends up on the kitchen bench, and I know that each and every one of those morsels of food has had its needs considered from the moment it has been shaken from a seed packet.

Care

Fruit and vegetable plants need tending. The universal allotment style of gardening that proliferates around the world is a testament to the love and care that need to go into growing food. Allotment gardening is where people without enough land of their own come together on a common patch and invest in their own little section of it. It started when there was mass migration to cities, so that country people could still grow their own food once they had moved into town housing with no yards. In the modern era, it has survived and flourished, creating communal green and productive spaces where the spirit and joy of productive gardening is shared among its participants in an environment where they can all learn from, and help, one another. It is also a testament to the joy it brings, both individually and on a collaborative level.

Understanding your plants' water requirements is very high on the list of things to do in successfully growing food. Vegetables are generally made up of more than 80 per cent water, so what goes in helps with the finished product. Different plants like to be watered in different ways. Tomatoes, cucumbers and zucchinis all like to be watered from underneath, which helps with any mildew and rot issues during the season. Lettuces love to be sprinkled from above. Carrots, when they're in the seed stage, need to be kept very moist. When our summer carrot seeds are sown, we will often water them four times a day or, if we are away from the garden, put soaked strips of under felt over them to keep them moist. The best way to understand your chosen plants' needs is to do a little reading on them, sift through a bit of contradictory advice and then have a go. Learn from your experiences each year and make notes, so that you don't repeat mistakes the next year.

Nutrition is another factor in successful care of your food plants. We check the pH and temperature of the soil, and are always on the lookout for when plants don't appear quite right. Again, the numerous ailments and setbacks are often specific to each plant and your own conditions, so it is always best to do specific research.

Our perennial crops need a whole different sort of care, on top of water and nutrition. Most of them need thinning out or pruning or training, or sometimes all three from year to year. These tasks are meditative and pleasing to the soul – knowing that you are helping something live healthily for many years, and, in return, getting produce, cuttings and rootstock that you can share far and wide.

Our fruit trees need care of a contrasting nature: proper pruning and spraying. I always reach for my trusty copy of *Reader's Digest* for pruning instructions, and am a devotee of spraying my dormant fruit trees with Bordeaux mixture. Bordeaux and Burgundy sprays can easily be made by the home gardener: the first with copper sulphate and lime, the second with copper sulphate and baking soda. All these ingredients are readily available.

The science of care of all plants, decorative and food crops both, is a vast, specialist subject. It is impossible to distil it into a few words of wisdom. Research will always help but, above all, you must be present for your plants. Take the time to notice them, especially if they are looking different or unwell. Follow that up with researching your findings so that you can help them.

The basic tenets of care for ourselves and our plants are: water, nutrition, protection. Plants are not so different from us, just requiring a slightly different version of these. And love; always a bit of love.

Pestilence and meteorological anomalies

Sometimes I think that the odds are cosmically stacked against those of us who want to make a difference to the planet by growing our own food. There are seasons when the weather is against you: too much rain or not enough rain, winds that strip produce away just as it is about to ripen. And there is a more modern phenomenon, which seems to have been induced by climate change: the disappearance of individual seasons. We have had years where winter seems to have stretched straight into summer, and winters that have not been cold at all. It is up to the individual to know the climate they are dealing with, and constantly make mental notes from year to year to help with contingency plans.

As well, you might have a plague of insects or have everything you grow devoured by marsupials or slugs. Then, of course, there are the cockies, who take great delight in snapping off garlic and broad beans in the spring, always reminding me that they represent the indigenous birds and this is not our land. It can be extremely discouraging, but there are many ways around these types of decimation. However, and unfortunately, protection of crops always comes at the expense of beauty. Nets, by nature, are not the most attractive garden feature.

Let's start with the slimy folk: snails and slugs. Because we have so many animals at Babbington Park, we try to use snail pellets as little as possible. While there are many brands on the market that are safe for cats and dogs, it's not something that we are sure about using, given our roaming fowl and with all the helpful insects, so we keep them to a minimum. Two methods that we have found to be very successful are the use of eggshells and of diatomaceous earth, a sand-type product made from fossilised algae that has a high silica content.

I end up with a large number of eggshells in the kitchen, which I store in a bucket in the refrigerator. When it's full, they are blitzed in the food processor with a little water. We then apply them to our salad greens and other crops that are susceptible to slugs and snails. As eggshells are natural, full of calcium and a waste product, we feel very confident about adding this to our soil. It also adds texture and breathability as beds are turned and re-used. The eggshells work so effectively because they are jagged and the gastropod family can't stand moving over them. Worms are fine with eggshells, as they can move around the sharp objects, but the more cumbersome slug or snail will just avoid them altogether.

I came across diatomaceous earth when I had the bad fortune of becoming infested with a parasite. My gastroenterologist was an open-minded and interesting man, and asked me if I would like to try a natural remedy, as I had not responded well to the standard medicines. I drank food-grade diatomaceous earth for a couple of weeks and, lo and behold, felt a great deal better. On researching this 'mud' that I was drinking each morning and evening, I discovered that it could be elevated to the 'very useful' status in many ways. It is particularly useful against the harder-shelled bugs that torment us, as it adheres to their exoskeletons and absorbs the liquid from them, dehydrating the bugs to a fatal level. It's also great for poultry, cattle and, dare I say it, when sprinkled on beds to use against fleas and bedbugs. Always travel with a little jar of diatomaceous earth, I say!

Another of our bugbears is the white cabbage moth, which has disastrous effects on the brassica crops. If you live in a farming area where canola is grown, the problem may become increasingly bad. The moths are particularly good at laying eggs on the underside of leaves and, when hatched, the little caterpillars are voracious eaters. With foliage being repeatedly damaged and eaten, the plant puts all of its energy into producing more leaves, rather than adhering to the task at hand of forming heads. If the caterpillars aren't dealt with, the plant will die, due to all of its leaves becoming skeletonised.

We use a number of methods to control these pests. First, our labrador, Moss, is trained to chase them. Also, we net all of our brassicas; when we are planting, all the brassicas and the rocket tend to be planted together, to make them easier to net. On top of this, the plants are sprayed. The most environmentally friendly solution is spraying with a commercially available deterrent, Dipel, which needs to be applied frequently. There are other options, like spraying with a solution of flour and water, which dries and suffocates the caterpillars, but this can be harmful to other insects. Companion planting, adding some oregano and land cress to the beds, has some effect in providing decoy crops for the moths, but we have found netting and Dipel to be the most effective remedy when used together. Our trusty eggshells are also extremely helpful when scattered in the soil to discourage any pupae that have been left on the ground.

Another odd thing about these moths is that they are terribly territorial and will not lay where another moth has laid. Decoy moths are easy to make out of white plastic shopping bags – attached to the end of sticks, they will often frighten off a 'rival'.

In an attempt to make our brassica bed less unattractive, seeing it lives under nets for at least eight months of the year, I have had a jig made, so that we can bend decorative steel hoops at will. These are placed at regular intervals throughout the rows, creating a firm framework to lay the net. We also search out black netting, which is far more pleasing to the eye.

Then, of course, we have the birds. Our avian friends can wreak havoc in a vegetable garden, especially when there are brightly coloured sweet things that lure them in. Our major bird attractors are the cane fruit and strawberry blocks. By our third year, there were over 650 square metres devoted to the various berries, which are a major attraction for the birds for more than six months of the year. While it would be delightful to be able to afford a proper permanent fruit cage, the budget hasn't quite stretched to that yet. Instead, we have the poor man's cage. Using star pickets driven into the ground, we use lengths of 5-centimetre poly pipe to form arches across them. These arches are then covered with black netting. The netting is small enough to deter birds and moths, but large enough to allow bees in so that they can execute their pollination rituals. This is a balancing act – if it is big enough to let the bees in, some predatory insects, like the harlequin beetle, can also get in – but we aim for a happy compromise.

Temporary netting structures can protect a multitude of plants. If you know you have problems with cockies, it is always advisable to net in the early stages of garlic and broad bean growth. This is reasonably easy: in the same vein as the fruit nets, we push stakes into the ground at regular intervals and make arches from a smaller-grade poly irrigation pipe. These structures can be removed once the danger has passed and the plants are robust enough to survive on their own.

In domestic gardens, blackbirds, starlings and sparrows can be a nightmare. I am not a believer in trapping birds to deter them, and I think that small-scale netting is a much more humane way to keep your fruit and vegetables safe.

Marsupials, rats, mice and rabbits can be another nightmare you need to contend with. At Babbington Park, we have no trouble with possums, but I know they do considerable mischief in city and suburban gardens. The only way to protect your fruit and vegetables is to create a structure around them that the possum cannot enter. More poly pipe and nets! The only good thing about the possum is that it is a nocturnal beast, so the nets can be removed during the day; this is especially important if you want your garden to look lovely for visitors. Another deterrent is motion-sensing lights that flash every time the possums move, but this could prove very irritating to your neighbours. Possums are easily trained to go somewhere else if it is too hard to access the food that you are growing.

You can also discourage rats and mice from entering the netting areas. We have had some terrible problems in the past, with mice being very highly active in our seed germination departments, and often eating all the pumpkin seeds before they have sent out any signs of life. Given the scale on which we germinate seeds, we have had some mesh frames made up that sit over our germination trays, but for the domestic gardener, re-using some of the inordinate variety of plastic packaging that fruit and vegetables are packaged in works very nicely. A seedling punnet or two will fit in one of those plastic containers that spinach comes in. They have drain holes, can act as a mini greenhouse for germinating seeds and are mouse-proof. Always be on the lookout in your domestic rubbish and recycling for containers that can be re-used in the garden.

In more rural areas, kangaroos and wallabies can do significant damage to fruit and vegetable crops. There are not many fences that can keep the roos out. We have learned to live with them and find most of the damage they cause is from their tails when they jump through the vegetables. We make wire cages to protect young fruit trees, and have discovered that our netted areas are of no interest to the roos. Given that they are mainly interested in grazing, they love the rich green grass that proliferates around the vegetable blocks, due to our watering regimens. Thankfully, we don't have a problem with wallabies, as they are much more interested in plants than grass.

We also don't have a battle with rabbits, but many people do. I would imagine that if we did, I would invest in a rabbit-proof fence. Rabbits' ability to dig and burrow under just about anything vexes many a gardener, and the best solution is to try to prevent them from entering your vegetable space. A chicken-wire fence of about 1.2 metres tall with 30 centimetres buried underground and the top bent over away from the garden, like a security fence, will help to keep them out. There is also quite a long list of plants they don't like that can be planted around the fence to discourage them. They are not fond of daffodils, lamb's ears, salvias, Russian sage, mint, parsley, tarragon or winter and summer savoury. In many instances, you could plant a lovely mixed border of bulbs, herbs and perennials, and no one would ever know that it was your rabbit-prevention technique.

Once you have kept all the pestilence at bay, there is the weather to contend with. Weather events are becoming more and more unpredictable each year. I always keep abreast of the weather fore-cast for the week, which gives me a little head start if there are unpleasantries on the horizon, be it heat, wind, cold or rain. I also have a working knowledge of the climate of my area. The internet is a wonderful tool for accessing the meteorological records of your region or area, which allows you to have an overview of average con-ditions all year round. In these times of change, this is really just a rudimentary knowledge tool, but it does help you predict and adapt better than if you were gardening without this sort of information.

There are some basic things to consider when you start planting your garden: mainly, siting and access to water. Flat, well-drained areas are desirable; productive gardening on terraces can also be delightful, but could involve costly earthworks. Access to water is an absolute necessity, as your garden will never thrive without it. Too much water, from inclement weather events, can be handled by drainage systems, if you are prone to flooding. Beds can also be cambered, to encourage run-off.

Wind can be one of the great destroyers. Our long-term goal is to have all the productive areas protected from the wind by hedging; in the meantime, we try to plant in ways that mean stronger crops protect the weaker. Tall crops, like corn, we try to plant in squares, so they are self-protecting, but we use their shadow in summer to protect delicate lettuce crops from the drying effects of the wind.

Frost is a natural part of our life here. I have had many crops destroyed by it, when a frost comes late and burns either the buffs off fruit trees or a whole row of early beans. It is the one weather pattern that I have grudgingly learned to accept, though. While many vineyards now have frost-sensing sprinkler systems to protect their grapes, I am prepared to accept frost, as it is part of the climate I live in. Somewhere out there, other forces are at work making sure that I appreciate what I do get to grow and not get complacent thinking that every year I will get everything I want. Nature just doesn't work that way.

Storage

What to do with all the food you have grown?

This is where my mantra of careful selection and control of the quantity of plants comes to the fore. Sustainability and seasonality go hand in hand. You don't want to grow so much of one thing that you miss out on other delights. Remember that there will be a progression of food all year long, especially if you have limited space.

Perhaps it is best if I move sequentially through the garden again, for my preferred storage options in the case of a glut:

The rhubarb is harvestable for at least eight months of the year. Quite frankly, I am always ready to have a little rest from it when winter comes. A lovely trick is to make some cordial at the end of the season, and you can sup it over the winter and think of summer.

All the berries freeze beautifully. We clean ours, pack them in ziplock bags and pop them in the deep freeze. The other tried and true preservation technique is to turn them into jam.

The currants and the gooseberries freeze well, but what I don't use fresh, I tend to put in the cordial, jam or jelly baskets. Homemade redcurrant jelly and blackcurrant jam are truly delicious. If I have an absolute abundance of blackcurrants, I will freeze some for sauces for duck or pork in the autumn and winter. The artichokes and asparagus I treat entirely as a seasonal crop. What we can't eat, I give away to those who don't grow either of them. The wonder of asparagus eaten as it is picked is impossible to describe. For me, it is one of the plants that most obviously suffers through packing and transporting; it seems to dehydrate even more quickly than the delicate cucumbers.

With all the annual crops, I tend to deal with them on a day-to-day basis, trying to grow what we need, as opposed to growing great quantities. There are a few exceptions to this rule. First, and, most importantly, there are the tomatoes. As we grow many varieties, I preserve them in different ways. With all the saucing varieties, I cook them down with a little basil and seasoning, put them through a Mouli and freeze. With the smaller varieties of tomatoes, I will often dry or semi-dry them and cover them with oil. Basil, I turn into pesto. If I have too much, I freeze it. Ready-made pesto freezes much better than fresh leaves; you'll know this if you have mistakenly tried freezing the latter and ended up with black mulch.

We grow a special sort of cucumber just for making cornichons out of – kilos and kilos of them, happily pickled in vinegar to last the year. Potatoes, we allow to dry off in the dark for a week or two, and then keep in saved sacks or potato bags. Onions and garlic, we tie up and hang from the rafters in the sheds. Pumpkins, we stack up somewhere cool and dry, and make sure we use them in order of their capacity to 'keep'. Corn, I strip from the kernels and freeze. Broad beans, I laboriously pod and peel, then freeze in containers of water, which helps to keep their vibrant green colour.

When it comes to the orchard fruit, I remember the lessons from my Malmsbury days. Some varieties of apples store better than others, and it is important to have knowledge about this so that you can store your crop appropriately. They like to be stored in the cool, on racks with good airflow. Quinces last for ages in similar environments. Pears can be picked hard and will ripen quietly, depending on the temperature. I tend to rack everything, as the fruit needs to be checked often to identify any that are blemished, as they will turn the whole lot. Stone fruit is best consumed from the tree, but makes excellent jam, chutneys and pickles. The D'Agen plums, we will try to dry as prunes.

I use the freezer a great deal more than I use anything else for preservation and storage of food. I am hoping to master the art of the Fowlers Vacola unit while I am at Babbington Park, but, in the meantime, I use the freezer. Traditional methods such as cool storage and root cellars are getting harder in these times of global warming, but it is not beyond the realms of possibility that, at some stage, I will investigate the construction of such a facility. Only time and yields will tell.

Recipes from the productive garden

THE KEY REASON for growing all this food is to eat it, which, as anyone growing food at home will know, is sometimes a double-edged sword. There is always the delight when produce first arrives in the garden, but there are also the times when you're dealing with a glut of it, which is a little more arduous. I approach the use of this wonderful bounty of fresh food by working through all the fruit and vegetables that we grow here. Some are used in basic preservation or cooking techniques; others are used in recipes.

Rhubarb and the soft fruits

Roast rhubarb

My favourite way to cook rhubarb is to roast it. Personally, I am not a fan of stewed rhubarb; it's always a little stringy for me.

The process of roasting rhubarb is simple. Clean the rhubarb by removing the leaves and cutting the bottom off from where you have pulled it from the crown. I grow a variety that doesn't need peeling, but, unfortunately, its name is lost in the mists of time. I then weigh the clean rhubarb, cut it into pieces the size that I need and place it in a bowl. I add half the weight of sugar to rhubarb (e.g. if I have a kilo of rhubarb, I would add 500 g of sugar), a little lemon and/or orange zest and juice, and half a vanilla bean. Give it a good toss, and then let it sit and macerate for about an hour. Place the rhubarb in a baking dish and roast until it is soft in an oven preheated to 180 °C. It will keep in the refrigerator for several weeks. I then use the roasted rhubarb as part of a compote of fruit, in meringue-based desserts like Eton mess or on pavlovas, and in crumbles, pies and tarts.

If you are wanting the perfect rhubarb pieces that you often see in fancy cake shops these days, the best way to make them is the sous vide method. Place your rhubarb pieces in a plastic bag with a little sugar and some aromatics (perhaps lemon rind and a piece of vanilla bean), remove the air and vacuum seal the bag. Cook at 61 °C in a water bath for about 45 minutes. I should note here that cooking fruit and vegetables by the sous vide method is one of the best ways to retain shape, texture and nutrients. However, it is not for me, as I cannot abide the single use of plastic the technique requires. I will always lean towards the more traditional style of cookery that employs reusability.

Raspberries, boysenberries, loganberries, blackberries, silvanberries and strawberries

The berry family – the sheer wonder of the first crop from each of these varieties is often replaced by the thought 'When are they going to stop?' So I have a little rule of thumb. When the first fruit of anything arrives and you are full of joy and wonder, take the minimal-intervention approach. Delight in a bowl of berries just as they are; or, if you are impatient like me, just eat them while you are out in the yard.

As the season progresses, you can start to use them in more complex ways. Jam is always a wonderful way to utilise a lot of the berries, as explained elsewhere. When you are a little over jams, that is the time to put berries in containers and freeze them. I can guarantee that, in the depths of winter, you will be very happy to pull some blackberries out of the freezer to add to a pie, or some raspberries to sit under a crumble. I can also guarantee that, no matter how sick of picking berries you were in summer and autumn, the joy of seeing the new fruit each year never diminishes.

Meringue roulade

Berry fruit works exceptionally well in meringue-based desserts such as pavlova or Eton mess, but my favourite is the meringue roulade. It always seems to be the easiest of these desserts to make, and it's a great presentation piece, which makes people very happy. Below are two variations: a plain and a chocolate version. The preparation after the meringue is cooked is the same for both. Spread it with whipped cream, or a mix of whipped cream and mascarpone, scatter with berries and roll it up. The rolling can be done in a tea towel, or in foil or cling wrap, the latter two giving a tighter finish.

SERVES 8

4 egg whites

250 g caster sugar

1 tsp white wine vinegar

1 tsp cornflour

extra caster sugar for dusting

Preheat the oven to 190°C.

Grease and line a 33 × 23 cm Swiss roll tin with baking paper.

Place the egg whites in a stand mixer and whisk at a medium-high speed until they have a firm peak and look creamy, whisking in sugar ⅓ at a time. Fold in the vinegar and cornflour.

Spread the meringue mix on the baking paper, smoothing the top. Place in the oven and bake for 10 minutes, then turn the oven down to 160°C and cook for a further 5 minutes.

Place a tea towel on the bench, cover with a sheet of baking paper, sprinkle with caster sugar, and then turn the roulade out onto the baking paper.

Cool for 1–2 hours.

The chocolate version
4 egg whites
a pinch of cream of tartar
200 g caster sugar
30 g Dutch cocoa powder
a pinch of good sea salt

Preheat the oven to 150 °C.

Grease and line a 33 × 23 cm Swiss roll tin with baking paper.

Place the egg whites and cream of tartar in the stand mixer, and whisk at a medium-high speed. Whisk the whites until they have a firm peak and look creamy.

Add ½ cup of the sugar gradually – around 1 tbsp at a time to start with, then 2 at a time as the mix becomes glossy and firm.

Sift the cocoa, salt and remaining sugar together, turn off the mixer, then add them all at once to the meringue at a low speed. Be very careful, so as not to be choked by a cloud of cocoa dust. Scrape the mix out into the prepared tray, in a large rectangular shape. Bake for 25–30 minutes until the top feels crunchy but not hard.

Place a tea towel on the bench, cover with a sheet of baking paper, sprinkle with caster sugar, and then turn the roulade out onto the baking paper.

Cool for 1–2 hours.

Crumble topping

A basic crumble recipe is always good to have on hand. This is one that started life as a topping for a cheesecake in a Nigel Slater recipe; over the years, I have adapted it to be my crumble topping of choice.

(However, being distracted by a good baked cheesecake topped with berries is not a bad thing either.)

200 g McVitie's biscuits
75 g unsalted butter
3 tbsp brown sugar
50 g jumbo rolled oats

Preheat the oven to 180 °C. Crush the biscuits to fine crumbs in a food processor, or in a sealed plastic bag with a rolling pin. Melt the butter in a small pan, add the brown sugar and cook, stirring, for a couple of minutes. Add the butter mix to the crumbs and the oats; mix thoroughly. Tip onto a lightly oiled piece of baking paper and place in the oven. Toast for 10 minutes, breaking the mixture up and moving it around a little. You are looking for the oats to be golden. I like my crumble topping a little clumpy, but if that is not for you, you can break it up quite finely. Remove from the oven, cool and store in an airtight container. I use this topping with fruit of all sorts; place the fruit in a shallow dish, then cover with the crumble topping and bake at 180 °C until bubbling.

Currants

There is no doubt that picking currants and preparing them for use is quite a fiddly and arduous task. I mainly use the whitecurrants and redcurrants as fresh fruit. They are great for garnishing Christmas-themed desserts and are also a lovely burst of tart/sweet notes in a summer salad. I am yet to have a glut of either of these colours, but when I do, I know that I will be making some redcurrant jelly.

The blackcurrants are a slightly different proposition. We brought some plants from the old garden, so they are producing well. When harvested, I always make a small amount of jam from them as a gift for my sister, as it is her favourite. I also like to cook some in a little sugar syrup and use it in Danishes made with my croissant dough and pastry cream. Cordial is the main use for the blackcurrants, as we serve it in the restaurant. I always tuck some away in the freezer. Blackcurrants are a delicious addition to a sauce with pork and duck; if they are frozen, I can pull them out at any time of the year and use them to enhance a sauce.

Globe artichokes and asparagus

I love that these two vegetables have a life where they only produce edible flesh for a few weeks of the year. They always remind me of what true seasonality is about: mid- to late spring, and the early weeks of summer, and then it is over. The plants are left flouncy and decorative, busy putting on new growth to produce more delights in the following year.

I tend to prepare all three sizes of artichokes that grow on each plant the same way. My method of choice involves picking them, cleaning them and then cooking them in the traditional Provençal manner: *Barigoule-style artichokes*. I start with a container of acidulated water (i.e. cold water with a lemon squeezed into it). Artichokes brown quickly once you start cutting them. I peel off all the outside leaves from the globe, chop the top off (usually about the top third) and then use a teaspoon to scoop out the 'choke'. Often it is easier to cut the artichoke in half first but, after a little practice, you should master doing the whole artichoke. After cleaning each of them, I lob them into the acidulated water and keep cleaning. Once they are all done, I sweat off some sliced onion and carrot in olive oil. Once it's softened, I add a couple of garlic cloves, a bouquet garni and 175 ml white wine. Bring it to the boil and burn off the alcohol. Add 200 ml olive oil, 250 ml stock or water, and 2 tbsp white wine vinegar. Bring back to the boil, add the cleaned artichokes, and simmer until tender. How long this takes will depend on the size. The artichokes can be kept in this liquid in the fridge for a couple of weeks. They can be used in salads and on pizzas, they can be crumbed and fried and dipped in aioli, or they can be stuffed and roasted. The liquid can also be strained, reduced and mounted with butter as a sauce, if you want to serve them absolutely in traditional Barigoule style.

Asparagus needs no such fuss as its high-maintenance mate, the artichoke. I never lose my sense of wonder at how delicious a spear of asparagus is when picked straight from the crown. The other amazing thing about asparagus is how well it pairs with some of the other delights of spring, such as eggs. The first flush of laying from my chickens in spring is always the most special egg production for me. I think it's because they lay so little in the winter that there is a feeling of being rewarded for all those mornings and nights I have fed them and let them out, and locked them up each night to keep them safe from the cold wet of the winter. Another precious spring thing is the emergence of the fine herbs – parsley, chervil, chives – all poking their heads up. Asparagus, eggs and fine herbs – a perfect match. Think of an asparagus omelette with a little Gruyère. Or maybe poached eggs, asparagus hollandaise and a scattering of herbs. My favourite is a dish that featured on the menu at Stephanie's Restaurant many years ago: lightly cooked asparagus, boiled or coddled eggs, and a dish of breadcrumbs fried in clarified butter with snipped fine herbs added. First, you dip your asparagus in the egg, and then roll it around in the breadcrumb mix – pure deliciousness.

Salads and leaves

We grow salad greens all year round. Deep in the winter, they grow slowly in the poly tunnel, but from spring to about June, they are planted outside. The two versions we grow are heading lettuces, including cos, butter, mignonette and oakleaf. There are also assorted cress and lettuces that we grow as cut-and-come-again.

Some of the heading lettuces – icebergs, Frisée and butter lettuces – are best grown out to maturity. This self-blanches the inside leaves, meaning they are sweet and succulent, with no trace of the bitterness that you find in the outer leaves. Other heading lettuces, like cos, oakleaf and all the frilly versions, are great for just picking the outside leaves off. It is fairly time consuming but means that a single lettuce will keep giving you leaves for months, if carefully managed.

The cut-and-come-again crops are harvested when the leaves are relatively small, and we generally get to cut three successive batches from them before the plant catches on and bolts to seed. We sow these varieties monthly, so we always have a fresh crop coming on. Once spent, they are lifted and fed to the poultry. These smaller leaves are often used in the restaurant, as garnishes for charcuterie plates, or as part of composed salads. Larger leaves are used for green salads. I often make a feature of the entire lettuce.

My preference is that a good green salad always accompany a meal, but this may not be the same for everyone. If you do like a green salad, it can be dressed with something as simple as a sprinkling of salt flakes and a slosh of good olive oil. However, my favourite dressing is a little more piquant than that, and I think my vinaigrette recipe stems from a childhood love of avocado vinaigrette.

Simple vinaigrette

1 part sherry vinegar
1 part extra virgin olive oil
2 parts grape seed oil

This is a dressing I use all year round; I do fiddle with it at times, though. If I have a salad that incorporates walnuts, I swap out the olive oil for walnut oil; if I'm using hazelnuts, I'll do the same substitution but with hazelnut. To make a creamier-style dressing that is lighter than mayonnaise, I whisk some of my sherry vinaigrette through sour cream or thickened cream. This is delicious on a salad made from a whole butter lettuce, sprinkled with snipped fine herbs. My salad leaves also get used in some substantial meat-based salads – I make a delicious warm sausage salad, for example. Leaves of the bigger variety get paired with pan-fried slices of Toulouse sausage, pan-fried potatoes and bacon, fresh tomatoes and sourdough croutes. For this salad, I use a lovely Dijon dressing, which I make by whisking in a slosh of vinegar to a big spoonful of mustard, and then whisking in grape seed oil until it thickens.

Salad leaves are for all year round, in my book. Dressings can come and go and change with the seasons, but one of the things many of the restaurant customers say is that they can't believe how delicious our lettuces are. It always reminds me that a well-grown lettuce, picked freshly and dressed pleasantly, can be something worth remembering.

Spinach

After many years of failing to grow spinach, I have finally succeeded. This has come about because of changes made to our sowing techniques. I had always tried sowing spinach directly into the ground, but now we raise it as a seedling in trays, and this is much more successful. Spinach is another plant that can keep giving if you just pick the outer leaves every other day.

Perpetual spinach and chard

This has proved much easier to grow than regular spinach, and is a cross between regular spinach and silverbeet. Its flavour and texture are coarser than English spinach and it is not good for eating raw. I use it in the same way I use chard. For example, in autumn, I make a lovely free-form tart using chard and goat's cheese, with a wholemeal pastry. Thankfully, the recipe uses a lot of chard – a prolific grower.

Chard galette

SERVES 6

pastry (make with 65 g butter, 250 g flour, a pinch of salt, 1 egg,
    65 g olive oil and enough water to bind)

2 large onions

2 tbsp olive oil

2 tbsp sugar

1 large bunch Swiss chard

500 g fresh goat's cheese

2 fresh eggs

salt and pepper, to taste

½ tsp nutmeg

enough pine nuts to sprinkle across the surface

olive oil

To make the pastry, rub the butter into the flour and salt, make a well in the centre and add the egg, oil and a splash of water. Bring together into a dough, and add a little more water if needed. Wrap in paper and refrigerate for 20 minutes or so. Roll out the pastry into a flat square or rectangle and place on parchment in a baking tin.

Prepare the caramelised onions by slow-cooking sliced onions in olive oil; once the onions are softened, sprinkle with sugar and continue cooking until browned and sweet. Let cool.

Trim chard leaf from the stalk; use only the large green leaves. Wash and place wet leaves in a hot, dry pan to wilt slightly.

Place a layer of the chard leaves over the pastry; it's okay if they extend over the edges.

Mix the goat's cheese, eggs, salt, pepper and nutmeg together, and place in the centre of the chard. Spread about 2–3 cm thick and form a square (approx. 30 cm) or rectangle.

Cover the surface of the goat's cheese with the onions.

Sprinkle with pine nuts. Fold the pastry and chard over the edges of the goat's cheese, and brush the pastry and exposed chard with olive oil.

Bake in a hot oven at 200 °C for 30 minutes or until the pastry is completely brown on the bottom. Remove, let cool, and serve at room temperature.

The fruiting vegetables

The fruiting vegetables comprise one of the most varied collections of things that we grow. Some are seasonal; some will grow all year round. I find that we don't tend to grow a lot of brassicas in summer and autumn, as there are so many other things to choose from and brassicas can manage in the winter. Here are some seasonal recipes, suggestions and tips for many of the vegetables we grow.

Broad beans

We have planted broad beans in the autumn and the spring over the course of our time here at Babbington. It must always be remembered that our growing climate is much colder than that of many other places in Victoria, so we are always a little later with our cropping. Our general rule of thumb is if the autumn plants fail to thrive, we will sow a replacement crop in early spring. One of the main reasons we grow them is that they are very good for the soil, fixing massive amounts of nitrogen. A word of caution: when it comes to preparation, broad beans are one of the most labour-intensive crops we grow, so I have learned to limit my sowing so that I am not overwhelmed by them. It is the time it takes to pick, pod and then double peel them that flattens my enthusiasm. But broad beans are one of the first things to produce after a long, cold winter, so, at the beginning of the season, they are welcomed with pure joy.

My basic method of *Preparing broad beans* is to pod the beans and then bring a pot of water to the boil. In the beans go, briefly – usually just till the water comes back to the boil – and then I strain them and run them under cold water, to stop the cooking process. I then slip them all out of their outer casings. Once this is done, I store them under cold water for a day or two.

If I know I am not going to be using them straightaway, I will freeze them in containers, submerged in water. Once they are at this stage, they can be added to whatever you desire. They pair beautifully with their spring cousins, the pea and the new seasonal herbs. They also love good parmesan, so pasta and risotto are two perfect dishes for broad beans.

Toss the broad beans with your salads; I like them with white meats, such as pork and chicken. Or splash out and make a dip with them. If I'm doing this, I love having the luxury of being able to mash them with white/slightly immature garlic – a sublime combination.

The beans themselves are not the only edible part of the broad bean plant; the tips are also delicious. I realised this when, one year, our broad beans completely failed in setting any pods. To feel a little better about the situation, I picked the top shoots and stirred them with a little garlic, olive oil and flaked salt. They have a delicious nutty flavour.

Peas

We are able to grow peas in spring and autumn in Lyonville, as it is so cold, which is an absolute treat for me. I love peas, but only when they are small and sweet and tender. I find the best way to deal with them is, once they start to become nicely formed in their pods, to pick them often. I will go up and down the row of peas every day. Once picked, I pod them and blanch them very quickly if I'm not using them right away. So, I am a bit fussy about my peas and don't enjoy them if they get too large; I find that the first couple of flushes of pods are the best. As the season wears on, I do successive plantings so I never have to pick mealy peas.

It is rare that I ever grow enough peas to make a real feature of them in the restaurant; but one year, with very kind spring weather, we were able to pick from the sown peas and from the pea mulch that was across the whole garden. That weekend, I served an entree of chicken boudin blanc on petits pois à la Française and it is one of my personal standout moments in the restaurant. I will always sow some iceberg seeds in August, so the lettuce coincides with the peas.

Petits pois à la Française

SERVES 8 AS A SIDE DISH

250 g kaiserfleisch, cut into lardons

6 spring onions, white part only, trimmed, halved

80 g unsalted butter, coarsely chopped

500 g baby peas

60 ml chicken stock

¼ iceberg lettuce, shredded

Heat a frying pan over medium-high heat, add kaiserfleisch and fry until golden (3–4 minutes). Add onion and butter and stir occasionally until onion is tender (3–4 minutes). Add peas and stock, bring to a simmer, add lettuce and simmer until the lettuce is tender and the liquid is reduced to coating consistency (3–4 minutes). Season to taste and serve warm.

Zucchini

Because we plant all our zucchini in the poly tunnel, we are assured of a long season. As with some other vegetables, there is a point when you cannot look at a zucchini again. The first zucchinis are very exciting and welcomed with open arms; the last may end up in the chookyard.

I use zucchini differently across the four to five months that they are producing. Early in the season, I pick them very small and may grill them or leave the flowers on; stuff the flowers, lightly batter and deep-fry them. By mid-season, one of the ways I can use up a lot of zucchinis is to cut them in a fine julienne and toss them with spaghetti, garlic, basil and olive oil. I will also make fritters with them. Further into the season, I will make delicious zucchini soup and a lovely lemon and zucchini cake. Somewhere in there, I also make this delicious zucchini relish.

Zucchini relish

750 g sliced zucchini
250 g peeled, seeded and diced tomato
150 g diced onion
2 cups sugar
375 ml white vinegar
1 bay leaf
a pinch of peppercorns

a pinch of cumin seeds

½ cinnamon quill

3 whole allspice

Prepare all the vegetables, then set aside. Bring the sugar and vinegar to the boil with all the aromatics, and boil for 5 minutes. Add the vegetables, return the saucepan to the boil and then simmer. Cook until the liquid is quite syrupy. Bottle in clean jars.

Zucchini soup

The important part of this recipe is keeping the zucchinis' colour. Treat the zucchini with respect: blanch it lightly in the liquid and puree immediately, to retain a vivid green.

SERVES 4

1 tbsp olive oil

1 onion, sliced

2 cloves fresh garlic, crushed

2 cups vegetable stock or water

6 small zucchinis, thinly sliced

1 cup spinach (optional)

10 basil leaves

sea salt and pepper, to taste

Heat oil in a large pot and sauté the onion and garlic over low to medium heat until they are translucent.

Add the vegetable stock and season to taste. Bring to the boil, then turn down heat and simmer for 10 minutes; add the zucchini, spinach and basil. Return the pot to the boil, until the zucchini is just cooked: a couple of minutes, at the most. It is always best to puree the vegetables first and add back the liquid to get the desired consistency. Serve.

Zucchini and lemon cake

This is a cake that is made with oil rather than butter. I am growing increasingly fond of these cakes, as they stay fresh for days and are more adaptable to making vegan: just replace the egg with egg substitute and don't put butter in the icing.

1 cup caster sugar
zest of 2 large lemons
1 cup vegetable oil
3 large eggs
¼ cup freshly squeezed lemon juice
2 tsp pure vanilla extract
2 cups all-purpose flour
½ tsp baking powder
2 tsp baking soda
¾ tsp salt
2 cups finely grated zucchini

For the glaze
3 tbsp unsalted butter, melted
1 cup icing sugar
½ tsp pure vanilla extract
2 tbsp freshly squeezed lemon juice

Preheat the oven to 180 °C, or use the baking setting. Spray a Bundt pan or 23 × 33 cm baking pan with non-stick cooking spray.

In a large bowl, mix together the sugar and lemon zest until the sugar is moistened and the zest is thoroughly incorporated.

Add in the vegetable oil, eggs, lemon juice and vanilla extract, and combine with a hand mixer on medium speed until all of the ingredients are incorporated.

In a separate bowl, whisk together the flour, baking powder, baking soda and salt.

Gradually add the flour mixture to the wet ingredients and mix until just combined. Fold in the zucchini.

Spoon the mixture into the prepared pan. Bake a Bundt cake for 45–50 minutes and a 23 × 33 cm cake for 35–40 minutes, or until a tester inserted into the centre comes out clean. Allow the cake to cool completely.

In a medium bowl, prepare the glaze by mixing together the melted butter, icing sugar, vanilla and lemon juice. Whisk until smooth and drizzle over the cooled cake. The glaze will harden slightly.

Beans

Next to potatoes, beans are my favourite vegetable – which is a bit unfortunate, as my vegetarian wife doesn't really like them. We grow mainly bush beans, the varieties that don't need trellising, planted successively for three or four months, depending on the conditions. If we are in for a mild, wet summer, I tend to plant more of them, as they struggle if it is too hot and windy. We also grow a small amount of climbing beans, but the bush beans are my favourite to cook with. In a good year, they can be prolific; so much so that if I had an ordinary household, I would have way too many. Growing and harvesting beans for a restaurant that feeds over 120 people a week is another task altogether. It involves a lot of picking on your hands and knees!

We have, on occasions, grown two different varieties of beans: the little green Flagrano, and a Tarbais-style bean destined for cassoulet. These are what is known as podding beans – they can be used as a fresh bean, as you would use a pea, or they can be dried for later use. While our crops have been successful, no one has ever found the time to pod them all, and they have ended up going back into the compost. I feel it may be one of my retirement jobs to perfect the art of shelling and drying beans.

Green beans cause me no such worries. I love them just lightly blanched. Again, growing your own gives you a product that is far superior to anything you can buy, and you get to control the size at which you pick them. I harvest them quite small and tender.

If you want to jazz them up a bit, blanch the beans and toss them in some foaming brown butter to which you can add some flaked almonds. Sprinkle with salt and enjoy. Too, they are particularly delicious if mixed in a little white miso and scattered with sesame seeds. I like them best of all with potatoes tossed in duck fat, garlic and parsley, and a confit duck leg.

Tomatoes

Given the cool climate we live in, a lot of our tomatoes are grown inside the poly tunnel. I will always submit to temptation and plant some field tomatoes, but they are often disappointing. We grow specific varieties based on what we know will succeed and are suitable for use in the restaurant kitchen. We lean towards a lot of pretty little cherry and pear varieties, as they grow well in our conditions; some middle-size tomatoes, particularly a variety called Jaune Flamme, which is a prolific orange fruit; and the two larger varieties we lean towards are Rouge de Marmande, a large red cooking one, and San Marzano Roma. I will always pop in a couple of beefsteak varieties, but they are only for home use. In caring for our tomatoes, we often pick them when they start showing some colour and ripen them on racks. This can be quite a time-intensive process, but I find it keeps the plants a little healthier, with less weight burden and fewer tomatoes being attacked by insects on the vine.

There are so many things that we do with our tomatoes, but I do have some favourites. I keep the bulk of the Rouge de Marmande and San Marzano crops by cooking them. I chop them roughly, then heat a large, heavy-bottomed sauteuse pan with a little oil. I then add the tomatoes and a couple of sprigs of basil, salt and a little pepper, bring them to the boil and then turn it down to a simmer and cook until much of their water has evaporated. I then use one of my favourite pieces of kitchen equipment: I put all of it through the Mouli. This removes most of the seeds and all the skin. I then either use the sauce, known colloquially as 'red sauce', or freeze it in buckets, or put it in jars and boil them, fully submerged, for 45 minutes.

With smaller tomatoes, I like to use them this way: I cut them in half and sprinkle generously with salt, olive oil and crushed garlic. I then allow them to macerate for at least half an hour. After that, I may toss them with fine raw ribbons of zucchini and sit them with baked white fish, or cook them down in a pan and serve them on spaghetti; the salt and the oil draw out so much flavour. If I have perfect beefsteak tomatoes, I will slice them thinly, salt them and eat them on toast for breakfast.

Capsicums

Capsicums are relatively new to my growing repertoire. A couple of years ago, I popped a few punnets of small red and yellow varieties in the poly tunnel. They were very good performers, so, each year, I put in more of the same. I usually end up buying seedlings, as I seem to struggle to raise capsicums from seed.

Our peppers are used extensively in ratatouille, and I also often make *Piperade*, which is a specialty of the Basque and Gascony regions of France. For this, I sauté some sliced onion with a little garlic in olive oil until soft, and add a good pinch of Espelette pepper.

Then I add strips of our colourful peppers. Traditionally, piperade is made with green peppers, but I use what I have on hand. Then I add either some peeled and seeded tomatoes, or some of my 'red sauce', which is always around at that time of year. I cook it down until the peppers are soft and the liquid has reduced away. Then I correct the seasoning and serve with grilled or roasted fish, poultry or meat, or as a vegetarian side. It is even delicious in an omelette with a little of another Basque great: some grated Ossau-Iraty.

Cucumbers

We grow two completely different cucumber crops. One crop is so that I can make my own cornichons, as I find the commercial brands a little sweet for my taste. For these, we grow either National Pickler or Paris double-yield varieties. Once they start fruiting, we make sure we go up and down the plants with a fine-tooth comb. No matter how carefully we look, though, we will always stumble across an enormous one that we have missed.

Cornichons

MAKES 2 L CORNICHONS

60 × 5-cm pickling cucumbers (about 1 kg) (up to 70)

65 g coarse salt

1 L cold water, plus an additional 375 ml

750 ml best-quality white wine vinegar

1 tbsp sugar

4 large sprigs fresh tarragon

3 cloves garlic, peeled (optional)

½ tsp whole black peppercorns

2 bay leaves

Trim off the stem ends of the cucumbers, wash away the little black spines, then rinse and drain. In a large bowl, combine the salt with 1 L water. Stir until the salt is dissolved, add the cucumbers, and let stand in a cool place for 6 hours. Scald two 1-L jars, lids and rings with boiling water and drain well. Drain the cucumbers, discarding the salted water that has been used. In a medium-size saucepan over medium heat, combine the vinegar, 375 ml water, and the sugar, and bring to the boil. Layer the jars with the drained cucumbers, herbs and spices, making sure to divide the ingredients evenly between the jars. Pour the boiling vinegar, water and sugar mixture into the jars, letting a bit of the liquid overflow the jars; this helps seal the lids well. Wipe the rim of each jar and seal. Let stand until cool. Store in a cool place for at least 3 weeks before serving. Refrigerate after opening.

The other crop we grow is eating cucumbers. I particularly like the small Lebanese varieties, ones that I can pluck and munch on as I go about my chores and that are also great for making summer salsa for home or the restaurant. My favourite version of this I refer to as 'my *Gazpacho salsa*'. With this one, I chop red and yellow peppers, cucumbers, a little purple onion, different coloured tomatoes and avocado (not from my garden!) into a small dice. All this is tossed together with salt, olive oil and sherry vinegar.

Eggplant

I had never realised how vicious an eggplant plant was until I grew them. The bushes are covered with long spikes that cause incredible pain if they lance you. Again, though, a homegrown eggplant is far superior to a shop-bought one. When you start growing different varieties, you get to experience a whole new world of pleasure.

The eggplant has a long and proud history in a variety of cuisines, which goes back millennia. My favourite variety to date is the pretty candy-striped one; its flesh is crisp and white to cut, but when cooked has the most beautiful creamy texture.

Eggplants feature widely in Japanese and Indian cuisines, and are great in curries or roasted with miso. I love them cooked on the grill and pureed with garlic and olive oil, whether as a dip or with lamb. And, of course, they are another basic ingredient of ratatouille.

Ratatouille

In late summer, early autumn, I am usually very flush with tomatoes, eggplants and capsicums, so out comes the ratatouille. I make this in a rather non-traditional way. I also just judge the proportions of vegetables based on the size of what I have; homegrown vegetables don't always conform to two of this and four of that. I like to cook the vegetables separately in a frying pan with a bit of oil, and then cook them down together in some of my 'red sauce'.

If using standard-size vegetables, I first chop an onion and crush a clove of garlic. Then I sauté those gently in olive oil until soft: about 10–15 minutes. While they are cooking, I cut about four zucchinis, two eggplants and two each of my small red and yellow peppers into 1-cm dice, keeping them all separate. I tip the cooked onion into a colander placed over a bowl, so I can re-use any oil. Then I place the pan back on the heat, add more oil, and toss the zucchini over a high heat until it's coloured. Place it in the colander with the onion mix. Place the pan back on the heat, add a little more oil, and toss the peppers over high heat until they are coloured. Place in the colander. Return the pan to the heat, add some more oil and the eggplant, then pour over the oil recovered from the other vegetables. Cook until golden brown. Place all vegetables in a pot, add an appropriate amount of 'red sauce' and cook slowly for 45 minutes to an hour.

Corn

Corn is not found often in French farmhouse food. It is a crop that is often grown simply as animal food in France. We grow a little at Babbington Park, but I find the low yields per plant versus its needs for water and food a little annoying. If we happen to harvest a good crop, I will often be at a loss as to what to do with it, and cut the kernels off the cobs and freeze them for when inspiration strikes me. Having said all that, when we were open for breakfast in the early days, one of the staples of the breakfast menu was *Corn fritters* served with bacon and oven-roasted Roma tomatoes.

To make this, I would take my favourite pancake recipe and add blanched corn kernels, chopped spring onion, chopped parsley, chopped dill and a little salt and pepper. The secret to making them perfect was to cook them in clarified butter.

Pumpkin

After years of successful pumpkin harvests at Malmsbury, my pumpkin growing hasn't been so flash at Babbington. I was quick to blame the climate, until Daniel Collings, who used to live here, told me that they grew wonderful pumpkins. I shall not be deterred, though. I do love growing the little Golden Nugget pumpkins, which are great to stuff and also have a lovely neat growing habit. The bushes take up only about 75 square centimetres, and the pumpkins form close to the stalk, making them a great plant for smaller gardens. Of the bigger varieties, I am particularly fond of the French and the

Italian warty varieties, Galeux d'Eysines and Marina di Chioggia. Both have delicious flesh and interesting skin.

My main approach to pumpkin is to roast it: either on the skin in wedges, or skinned and cubed. I will often pair it with lamb or fill crepes with a mixture of pumpkin and ricotta, or serve the roasted pumpkin atop gnocchi Parisienne.

Gnocchi Parisienne with roasted pumpkin and sage butter

SERVES 4

135 ml water

90 g butter

2 tsp salt

1 cup flour

3 eggs

½ cup grated parmesan

1 tbsp Dijon mustard

1 kg firm pumpkin, butternut or Queensland blue, peeled,
     cut into 1.5-cm dice

60 ml olive oil

200 g unsalted butter

⅓ cup sage leaves

shaved parmesan to serve

Bring the water, butter and salt to the boil, making sure the butter is melted before the water boils. Stir in the flour as you would for choux pastry. Cook and stir until the dough comes away from the sides of the pan. Remove from heat and put in a stand mixer or a mixing bowl. Cool for 5 minutes.

With the paddle attachment fitted to the machine, or with a wooden spoon, add the eggs, one at a time, and then the cheese and mustard.

Bring a large pot of salted water to the boil. Turn down to a simmer. Place the gnocchi dough in a piping bag with a plain ¾-cm nozzle. Working quickly, squeeze the dough from the bag into the water, cutting it off with a small knife every 2 cm. Continue till you have done ¼ of the mix. The gnocchi will rise to the surface; simmer for about 3 minutes and then lift out into an iced water bath. Continue in this manner until all the dough is used. The gnocchi should then be drained and tossed in a little oil. It can be kept like this in the refrigerator for 3–4 days.

Preheat the oven to 200 °C.

Toss the diced pumpkin in olive oil, place in a baking dish in a single layer and bake till soft and slightly caramelised (about 20 minutes).

Place the gnocchi in an ovenproof serving dish, scatter with the pumpkin and return to the oven until puffy and golden (about 15 minutes).

When it is nearly done, place the butter in a small saucepan, cook over a low heat for 4–5 minutes until the butter starts to turn brown, and add the sage leaves. Cook for about 1 minute or until crisp; make sure the butter is a lovely nutty brown.

Remove the gnocchi from the oven and pour the butter and sage leaves over it. Garnish with curls of parmesan.

The Brassica family

Over the years, I have learned so much about which plant belongs to which family simply through what the seed looks like. This is how I learned about the vastness of the Brassica family and how much respect it deserves. The family covers a huge range of day-to-day salad varieties, fruiting vegetables and root vegetables. The seeds are small, round and brown. They appear innocuous, really, with many looking very much the same. It is only once planted and thriving that they tell the story of who they really are.

Mustard greens, mizuna, mibuna, tatsoi and rocket

This grouping is of some of the leaves that we grow for our salad mixes. It doesn't even include a huge range of Asian greens that I don't use that much, but bok choy, pak choi and their cousins also belong to this family. We plant many successive crops of these across nearly the entire year. As well as being incredibly varied, the Brassica family is super resilient to weather changes. They may be a bit slower to grow in winter and a bit quick to bolt in high temperatures, but, most of the time, all these leaves provide us with three cuts of salad greens.

Broccoli, brussels sprouts, cauliflower and cabbage

These four are another mainstay of our crops. While we sow them as seeds over a six-month period, they are vegetables that I use mostly in the cooler months. I find that they are some of the only things that can survive the cold winters here, and there are a couple of varieties that come into their own during the hungry gap months – that is, the bit of spring before the asparagus, peas and broad beans are ready but with little else having survived the winter. The sowing time of some of these plants is critical, as they need to do a lot of growing in the warmer months to be able to provide once the temperature starts to plummet. The two standout examples are brussels sprouts and purple sprouting broccoli (PSB). We start the sprouts in October and the PSB in November. We may not get sprouts until, at the earliest, May, but they are worth the wait. The PSB takes even longer. It has amazing foliage for months and months and then, bang, just like magic, in late August/early September it starts to throw out copious amounts of purple heads, and goes on and on for months. If I can't use it all in the restaurant, we maintain a weekly picking regimen anyway, just to keep it from going to seed and to keep the plants producing. The excess goes to our fruit and veggie man two doors down from the restaurant.

Broccoli, I cook simply: steamed or boiled. Sometimes it is tossed in a pan with oil or butter, sometimes with almonds added. I also love to roast broccoli in a hot oven with a little olive oil and a sprinkling of salt flakes. Small heads of broccoli are delicious tossed with pasta, garlic, olive oil, chilli and crushed anchovy.

Brussels sprouts, I give a little more love to; after all, I tend them for a long time. Growing your own means that you can pick them when they are much smaller than the commercial ones. Give them a quick boil and then throw them into a pan where you have crisped up some bacon lardons. I also like to add some coarse breadcrumbs, so that there is a crunch in the texture profile. For vegetarians, the pairing of brussels sprouts and hazelnuts is just as good; here I would also add a little splash of hazelnut oil. If you have many brussels sprouts to play with, they are delicious shredded and dressed in olive oil, lemon juice and salt. Then there are the pasta and gnocchi dishes I cook where I dismantle them into their individual leaves and toss them over the heat so that they are just wilted through the other ingredients. No one should shy away from a sprout simply because of bad memories of, say, overcooked ones. They are delightful.

Then come the cauliflowers. We have grown many of these: white, green, purple and Romanescos. I won't bother with the purple ones again, as they look magnificent when raw but are very unattractive when cooked. We will always grow the other three, though. We do like to look after the white ones with special care; once the head starts to become well formed, we tie the leaves together so that the plant isn't affected by the sun, rain or frost.

I am a great fan of roasted cauliflower, often with the addition of North African spice mixes such as chermoula. Sometimes I will chop the cauliflower into pieces and sometimes roast it whole as a presentation piece. Another family favourite is cauliflower sliced, crumbed and fried, and served with katsu sauce. On a more restaurant-based theme, I love making a cauliflower puree, for which I cook the cauliflower in milk and puree it. This is delicious under a winter salad. Think of it with pan-fried Toulouse sausages, crisp-roasted cauliflowerettes, mustard greens and hazelnuts. The puree is also delicious served as a small soup course.

And then there are the red and green cabbages, imperial beasts in the vegetable garden. There is nothing more heroic than a bed with a double row of cabbages in full leaf. They take up a ridiculous amount of room for such a 'cheap' vegetable, but I love them. Green cabbage – we grow savoys – I use a lot with pork and duck. I treat it very lightly: shredding it, lightly blanching it, and then tossing it in a pan with butter or pork or duck fat. I love to maintain a little crispness and brightness. As well as going very well with these two meats, cabbage is very good friends with Dijon or grainy mustard.

Purple cabbage, I cook a little differently. My method of choice is to shred it, cook it down in a little olive or grape seed oil, and then add some red wine vinegar. This is another perfect accompaniment to pork and duck, and the addition of some pan-fried apples completes it.

Cabbage is also delicious raw, although I have discovered that it upsets some people's stomachs. I love to create different sorts of slaws for both home and the restaurant. Purple cabbage, raw beets and purple onions is a favourite, as is shredded savoy, green apple, snow peas, celery and walnuts. They are both dressed with appropriate vinegars and oils.

Cabbage skin is also wonderful to use as a wrapper for a package. Stuffed cabbage rolls are a staple of many national cuisines. They are often full of seasoned pork, but are just as delicious with a carefully crafted vegetarian filling.

Kohlrabi

Our planting kohlrabi happened by complete accident. I had never even cooked with it before. We had grown a leaf for our salad mix, the seed of which was labelled purple kale (yet another member of the Brassica family that can turn its hand to many things). It was great in our salads, but the row of plants got away from us and we didn't get back to pull it all out. It only took a few weeks for them to take off and, lo and behold, we were well on the way to growing beautiful purple kohlrabies. The plants themselves look a little like aliens but taste fantastic. They combine the texture of an apple with the flavour of a very sweet cabbage.

Having grown kohlrabies by accident, I had to do a little research into what to do with them. I found that they are great raw in salad and they are fantastic roasted. We love them so much that we now grow them specifically for cooking, not just to have a fancy salad leaf.

Radishes, swedes and turnips

I have always thought of these three as root vegetables but, with my learned respect for brassicas, I have now shifted my thinking about their family ties and how I use them. Radishes, we grow aplenty – almost all year round. My two favourites are French Breakfast radishes and their close cousin the D'Avignon. Both are pinky red with white tips, and the D'Avignon a little longer and faster growing. In ideal conditions, it will be ready for harvest in twenty-one days. These radishes we serve in a traditional French manner, with butter and salt. We also love to include them in salads. And there is a thing we do that many would not think of: radishes are delicious roasted. Their peppery nature is delightful when they are roasted for 10–15 minutes in a hot oven with salt and a little olive oil.

Another that we have become very fond of in recent years is the watermelon radish. This is a member of the daikon family, and is round with white skin. Under the skin, though, is a ball gown of bright pink or purple. They don't need to be peeled, just scrubbed, and are delicious raw or pickled, or can be roasted or mashed.

The final radish we grow is a proper long white daikon. We grow this not to eat but as a tillage crop. The idea is that the fast-growing daikons will grow straight down 30 to 40 centimetres and provide a wonderful non-intrusive way to break up the soil structure. We leave them in the ground to rot, top dress with compost and then plant on top of the undisturbed radish.

A little note about pickling any of the radish family: I am keen on a quick pickle, as I have never mastered the art of pickling radishes without them smelling. A jar of pickled radishes can put you off opening the fridge, as they really stink like flatulence.

Below is my go-to pickle, where I just do what I need to do first and then move on with cooking whatever the radishes are accompanying.

Quick pickle

125 ml apple cider vinegar
125 ml water
1 tbsp white sugar
1 heaped tsp salt flakes

Place the vinegar, water, sugar and salt in a small saucepan, and bring to the boil, stirring to dissolve the salt and sugar.

Pour over thinly sliced radish, onion or cucumber. Cool. Can be used in ½ hour.

The swede is not a common vegetable in either French or Australian cooking. It is eaten more in America, where it is known as rutabaga, and, of course, in Scotland, where it is known as neeps. Swedes are another food that is often fed to livestock; I adore their colour and sweetness, and always grow a small crop. They are great as a mash or a soup, and can add a lovely colour contrast to a plate of roasted vegetables.

Turnips don't always get the love that I think they should. They have a complex flavour that rides the brassica profile. They have a bit of heat, a bit of sweetness and a wonderful texture. My favourite is the fast-growing leaf turnip, or Japanese turnip. The leaves are delicate enough to be used in salads or, as the turnips get a bit bigger, they can be tossed in a pan. The small white globe of a turnip is perfect for lightly steaming and serving in a salad of baby root vegetables or dishes that involve broths, like pot-au-feu.

The root vegetables

Lyonville and its surrounds are famous for soil that is perfect for growing root vegetables, particularly carrots and potatoes. Our plot is no different and we excel at many root crops. Some, like our parsnips, have been a little trickier, but with each year, we are getting better at ironing out the wrinkles. We can feature root vegetables in the restaurant all year round. Along with the lettuce and salads we serve, it is the carrots that draw the most compliments from the customers. Simple pleasures can make people smile.

Beetroots

This is a vegetable that I have learned to like, as I had never really been drawn to it. When you grow your own produce, though, I feel you develop a compunction about eating and liking everything that you have raised, almost as a matter of respect.

We grow many sorts of beetroot: purple ones, candy-striped ones, yellow ones and white ones. The fascinating thing about beetroot seeds is that there are a few of them clumped together in the seed you plant. This is why when they grow, a few will grow together, no matter how carefully you spaced them out. I never bother to thin them and just let them grow in their clumps, as nature intended. A little like the correlation between brassica seeds, the same family traits can be found in silverbeet, chard and perpetual spinach seeds. Their seeds are a funny little cloud of interconnected lives.

Beets can be eaten cooked or raw. I love serving them with white dairy products, such as yoghurt or feta. They also seem to have a lovely symbiotic relationship with dill and garlic. For the meat eaters, I love the combination of lamb with beetroots. If I have larger beets, I may wrap them in foil and roast them whole, scrubbing the skin off after they are cooked. Or I may peel them, julienne them and add them to a salad. They also love to be pickled; a wonderful way to preserve them. This is from the CWA recipe book:

Pickled beetroot

1 kg beetroot, washed

1–2 cups of sugar (according to taste)

4 cups white vinegar

1 tsp ground cinnamon

1 tsp ground allspice

10 cloves

12 peppercorns

1 tsp salt

Cook the beetroot in boiling water, then peel and slice or dice and pack into sterilised jars.

Combine the remaining ingredients in a large saucepan. Bring to the boil, then remove from the heat.

Cover and allow to stand for 20 minutes, to allow the vinegar to cool a little and the flavours to infuse.

Strain and pour over the beetroot, making sure that the beetroot is well covered with the liquid. Seal immediately.

Historically, sugar beets were grown for sugar before the rise of sugar cane. Part of this family is the curiously named mangelwurzel – a variety that I grow for entertainment only. They reach an enormous size, often over 10 kilos, and are traditionally used as another fodder crop. Picked when they a little smaller, they are great for making a sweet, yellow mash out of, not unlike a mash made of swedes. I also sometimes use the leaves as I would silverbeet – wilting them down as a vegetable, or using them in quiches or tarts. But be aware that the *Beta vulgaris* family from which it comes has oxalic acid in the greens and the mangel leaves should only be eaten when young, as they become a little strident to the palate when older.

Carrots

I am never quite sure of how the carrots became my darling of the vegetable patch, but they have. I love them. I love them so much that I often wonder what they look like underground, all those lovely straight orange legs reaching ever downwards. I grow a few varieties: mainly Nantes, as a long carrot; and Paris Market, as a small, round carrot.

And for all my love of my carrots, I don't do very much to them at all. I generally make a side dish of *Tarragon roasted carrots* to serve with main courses. Once scrubbed, I never peel the carrots; they go into a baking tray with a little water, a good piece of butter, salt and tarragon. Then they go into an oven that has been preheated to 180°C, and will take between 20 and 40 minutes, depending on their size. Sometimes, though, I add a little honey and reduce the cooking liquor to use as a syrup.

Garlic

Growing garlic has been a little troublesome here at Babbington Park. I think it may be that it is just that little bit too cold and too wet. Still, each year, we try to, and do, grow a small crop. The size doesn't fuss me too much, as we have some wonderful people in less marginal climes near us who do specialise in growing a beautiful product.

Of all the ways to include garlic in cooking, I have two that always come up trumps.

The first is to use it as a natural grater, with bread toasted either in the oven or over coals, by running a clove of garlic over the surface of the bread. It is how I always prepare croutes for soups, and for some dips.

The second way takes a bit more work. I slice a whole bulb of garlic across the middle, drizzle it with a splash of olive oil, season with salt and pepper, and add a sprig of thyme. Then I put the bulb back together again, wrap it in foil and bake for 2–3 hours, until soft, in an oven preheated to 140°C. The garlic can then be used as a spread on crusty bread or as a wonderful addition to mayonnaise,

be smeared on cooked steak or served with a goat's cheese whip …
and on the suggestions go. Garlic is another one of what I feel are
deluxe products from the garden; simple yet elegant. If you do grow a
good crop of garlic, it allows you to use it with largesse when braising
meats and vegetables, throwing a handful of garlic cloves in at the
start of the cooking process. And on a decorative front, plaiting garlic
is a delightful pastime and pretty in the kitchen.

Leeks

I can never grow enough leeks; they should always be in the garden.
No matter what the variety and what the name on the seed packet
promises, we struggle ever to grow a leek that is as big as the ones
you can buy. However, what they lack in size, they make up for in
a flavour that is more perfect than you can imagine. Leeks take a
long time to grow, taking up space for six to eight months, but, gosh,
they are worth it. Imagine a perfect leek and Gruyère quiche; leek
and potato soup; brined and roasted chicken, with a creamy leek and
morel sauce.

Often we have lots of little ones, and my favourite way of preparing them is to clean the leeks thoroughly and then cook them in a
flat pan with salted water and butter. They can then be used as a side
vegetable or to decorate the top of a quiche.

Onions and shallots

Of the Allium family, it is shallots that we grow the most of, and
I have a predilection for what is known as a golden shallot. This is
a smaller variety and is slowly being replaced in the market by the
larger banana shallot, which is either purple or brown and coveted
for Asian and subcontinental recipes. The smaller golden shallot is

my choice because it is perfect for classics such as boeuf bourguignon and coq au vin.

They are fiddly to prepare: the smaller the shallot, the more need to be peeled. As a short cut when I am preparing many, I bring a large pot of water to the boil and dump all the shallots in. I then bring it back to the boil and strain, and, with a sharp paring knife, pop the shallots out of their skin. Once they are in this state, they are ready for adding to your favourite recipe. If I am cooking them as a side dish, I put them in an appropriately sized baking dish, with lots of butter, a little thyme and salt, and cook in the oven at 180 °C until soft and golden.

If I were using them for a *Shallot tarte Tatin*, I would half-cook them as described above, remove them from the oven, and deglaze the pan with vinegar. I would then place the shallots in an appropriate pan, so you have a single layer, pop a puff-pastry lid on top, and cook them at 220 °C until the pastry is done. Then serve with a crisp green salad. This is my idea of a luxury dish, as I know how much work goes into not only growing and harvesting the shallots but into preparing the dish.

Parsnips

I am learning to master the growing of parsnips; over the years, they have been a difficult one for me. I have given up on trying to grow proper celeriac parsnips, but I refuse to let this vegetable family beat me entirely.

My main problem is getting them to germinate properly. I have done endless research and tried many different methods suggested on the internet. Much to Kieran's and James's delight, I even tried germinating them in soil moistened with my own urine, as a champion parsnip grower suggested. It didn't work, and thus we didn't get to play with pissy parsnip alliterations. Recently, though, I have had a breakthrough. First, I keep my seeds in the fridge; second, I have been germinating them in cell trays and then planting them out. I tried this method because we have had some success in thinning out plants that have germinated and replanting them (yes, they are that precious), so I concluded that parsnips wouldn't mind starting life this way instead of by direct sowing. My last two sowings have had a 90 per cent germination rate, which brings a smile to my face.

Parsnips are a beautiful vegetable to cook. I treat them very lovingly, as once germinated, they can take up to eight months to mature. I care for them a great deal during their life in the soil, so I cook them with great respect.

A few of my favourite *Parsnip delights*: a little like the cauliflower, they make a beautiful puree if boiled in milk. I peel them, slice them, and then cook them in seasoned milk until tender, then whizz them till smooth. They are a classic roast vegetable and I have a great fondness for them roasted with pears. This combination can also make for a delicious warm salad if tossed with leaves, toasted walnut and a sharp vinaigrette, and placed on a puddle of warm parsnip puree. Another classic way of cooking parsnips is to take a vegetable peeler to their flesh and deep-fry those peelings at 170 °C till golden brown. Parsnip chips make a wonderful garnish for the aforementioned salad.

Potatoes

As we are in a potato-growing area, I don't try to grow potatoes for year-round use. I do find that there is a four-month gap in supply, and I try to cheat the seasons a little and grow enough potatoes to cover this gap. This means that we sow them earlier than the local farmers do, and keep them warm under lots of straw and fleece. We are then able to dig potatoes from about Christmas until April,

when the local ones start to come back in. We grow a number of different potatoes each year: Kennebec, Dutch Cream, Sebago, King Edward and Nicola, to name a few. None of them are outlandishly special, but their flavours are superior when cooked only hours after being dug from the ground.

I serve potatoes with nearly every main course that I have ever sent out at du Fermier: potatoes cooked in cream, potatoes cooked in stock, potatoes cooked in duck fat. Yet, it is a potato terrine entree that has stolen the show to become the favourite of all my potato variations.

Potato terrine with Gruyère and garlic

SERVES 8

1 tbsp butter, softened

3 eggs

1½ cups pure cream

1½ tsp flaked salt

½ tsp freshly ground black pepper

¼ tsp grated nutmeg

1.25 kg Nicola potatoes, peeled and very thinly sliced

3 cloves garlic, minced

225 g Gruyère, grated

For the salad

300 g baby salad leaves

1 pear

½ cup walnuts, lightly roasted and salted

25 ml sherry vinegar

25 ml extra virgin olive oil

50 ml grape seed oil

Preheat the oven to 180 °C.

Prepare a 30 × 7 × 7.5 cm terrine. Mould by greasing the pan with butter and lining it with parchment paper.

Beat the eggs together in a bowl, and whisk in cream, salt, pepper and nutmeg. Set aside.

Lay the potatoes in overlapping rows until the bottom of the dish is completely covered. Sprinkle with a bit of minced garlic and a handful of grated cheese. Repeat the layers until they are about halfway up the side of the dish. Pour half of the cream mixture over the potatoes, alternately lifting up the layers with a fork and then pressing down, to ensure that the cream gets between all the layers. Repeat layering the potatoes, garlic and cheese until it's all used up and you reach the top of the dish. Pour the rest of the cream mixture over the potatoes, once again lifting and pressing on the potato layers, to make sure that there are no dry spots.

Cover the dish with aluminium foil and bake for 1 hour. Remove the foil and bake for an additional 15–20 minutes, or until the top is golden brown and the potatoes in the centre of the dish are tender when pierced with a small knife.

The orchard

As our fruit trees are very young, we are at least two years away from starting to harvest any crops. Each of the varieties have been planted with specific purposes in mind.

Almonds

An almond tree is particularly beautiful – tall, upright, with lovely serrated leaves. It is usually the first tree to blossom and the last to harvest from. The best way to harvest almonds is to lay a tarp under the tree and shake the tree vigorously.

If you grow your own almonds, you can have a hard-to-come-by treat, as green almonds in spring are a curious delicacy. The outer shell is green and fluffy, telling us that it is more closely related to the peach than to other nuts, and the inner kernel is a soft, greenish, squishy thing. I have tried several recipes for green almonds and decided that they are not really to my taste, so I am prepared to wait till the outer casing has hardened and it becomes the almond I know and love.

Almonds are an indispensable part of my repertoire. I often use them in savoury concoctions, but mainly in desserts. I make praline pastes, frangipane mixes, meringues and cakes, to name only some. The precious few almonds that I will harvest from my own trees, I will, I think, just enjoy as a fresh nut.

Apples

Apples are the orchard tree that I am most drawn to, and I use the fruit across the spectrum of dishes that I cook in the restaurant. They are often found in my entree dishes and, in warmer weather, I will often add a julienne or batons of apple to salads.

One of my preferred methods is to make a salad of apple, a little fennel, watercress and cucumber. Dress it with a small amount of lemon juice and crème fraîche, and serve with cold or hot smoked ocean trout. As the weather cools, it is a great idea to cut your apples into eighths and cook them gently in clarified butter till golden brown. They are wonderful in a warm salad of smoked duck breast, with walnuts, a mix of sweet and bitter leaves and a sharp vinaigrette. If you have vegetarians at your table, the same salad is delicious with roasted beetroots instead of the duck.

Apple works beautifully with two of my go-to proteins: duck and pork. You can make a puree by cooking apples slowly in butter and then placing them in a food processor, which is a great way to start an elegant plated main course. You can place on the puree some red cabbage cooked with vinegar, scattered with sautéed apple pieces and some carefully sliced duck breast or pork loin, finished with a lovely sauce – I will often use a reduced veal stock sauce for dishes like this.

It is when combined with pastry, though, that apples really come into their own. The simplest such dish is a classic *Fine apple tart*. Cut a circle of puff pastry and then lay finely sliced apple in concentric circles. Add a few little dobs of butter, a sprinkle of sugar and cinnamon, and into a hot oven it goes. It is perfect served with vanilla ice cream and salted-caramel sauce.

The tarte Tatin has the same ingredients but is made a little differently. Pour caramel into the pan first, then lay out the apple in chunky circles, then add the puff pastry, bake and invert. Apple pies are another favourite, such as a pâté sucrée encasing beautifully stewed apples. I like to combine the apples I grow for pies, so that I use some varieties that stay firm and some that explode, so the filling has a terrific texture.

Breakfast can be a treat if you are having waffles, sautéed apples and maple syrup butter. And fruit mince left over from Christmas can be stuffed into a cored apple, and the whole apple baked and served with Armagnac custard. Apples are also great for making chutneys and relishes, and particularly good paired with beetroot.

Apricots

I always think of apricot trees as the personification of summer; the trees laden with golden orbs, warm from the summer sun. The reality of growing them is not so dreamlike for me. Of the two trees that

I had at Malmsbury, one fruited, but the other was riddled with a disease that we couldn't defeat. I am hoping that the couple we have planted at Babbington will do better, and I shall look ahead and aspire to realise my dreamscape.

My main kitchen purpose for apricots is to turn them into jam, a great favourite with customers. It is also a wonderful baking tool in French patisserie work, as the jam can be sieved and used as a glaze on all sorts of tarts and desserts, such as rum baba. Apricots are delicious on a frangipane tart and, like berries, go very well with a baked cheesecake. They can also be split and grilled, and served with a sprinkle of amaretti crumbs and mascarpone cream. On a savoury note, they are delicious roasted with duck or popped into a chicken tagine.

Cherries

We have planted two different types of cherries here: Morello cherries, the sour ones, and eating cherries. The Morello cherries I will preserve either in sugar syrup or in a pickling solution. The sweet ones will be used for desserts, and the pickled ones as a garnish for charcuterie plates, composed salads, and in meat and poultry sauces. We will have to wait for about five years for the trees to produce a bumper harvest.

I delight in using the eating cherries in clafoutis, a traditional French dessert that is really just a baked custard.

Clafoutis

SERVES 8

4 eggs

60 g caster sugar, plus extra for dusting

30 g plain flour

30 g cornflour

320 ml milk

320 ml thickened cream

1 tbsp Armagnac

20 g butter

250 g pitted cherries

pouring cream, to serve

Preheat the oven to 180 °C.

With a whisk, beat the eggs, sugar, flour and cornflour until thick and foamy. Gradually add the milk, cream and Armagnac, and whisk until well blended. This mixture can be made several hours ahead of time and refrigerated until you are ready to cook it.

Butter the sides and base of your chosen pan and dust with extra sugar; I use raw sugar, for extra crunch. Scatter the cherries evenly across the bottom of the pan, then carefully pour the batter over the fruit.

Bake for 45 minutes or until puffy, golden and done in the centre (if you give it a little shake, there should be no wobble); smaller ones will take less time to cook – about 20 minutes. Remove and allow to cool slightly, then serve with cream.

Chestnuts

Chestnuts are often the bane of an apprentice cook's life. They are not the simplest thing to prepare, and when growing your own, you are signing up for a next-level commitment to pain and hard work. First, I have to remove them from the very prickly conker to get the smooth brown nut. These are best slit at the bottom in the shape of a cross, popped in a hot oven and the nut removed. The nut then needs to have its seed coat removed, which is most effectively done by plunging it into boiling water and working quickly with a small paring knife to take off the brown skin. This makes double peeling broad beans seem enticing. The result is something special. Peeled chestnuts can be turned into a delicious soup, added to winter pasta dishes, or cooked with milk and sugar to create a sublime paste. They can also be cooked in syrup to become a marron glacé, the specialty of the Rhône-Alpes region of France. Once you've peeled your chestnuts, they need to be treated with reverence because of all the work it has taken to get to the point in preparation when you can cook them.

Chestnuts are ready to use in autumn, so I always mix them with other food that evokes an autumnal forest feel: quail, pork and mushrooms come to mind. They also have an important place in the pastry arena, but I find that I use my fresh chestnuts for savoury dishes and leave the pureed and sweetened versions to the expert chestnut growers. Producing a sweetened chestnut puree is too formidable a task for me, and our local growers have enough chestnuts to make commercial quantities, thus relieving me of a job I would be sure to fail at.

Figs

We are yet to see if our fig tree will cope in Lyonville. Planting the tree on a north-facing wall, where we can cover it to protect it from frost, may not be enough. But we will see. Even if she never bears fruit, she will be a beautiful specimen tree.

A perfect fig doesn't need much done to it. Serve with cheese or salami, or drizzle with honey and bake lightly.

Hazelnuts

Even though we have planted hundreds of metres of hazelnuts as a hedge around the productive garden, I am not convinced that I will ever harvest a large number of them. The sheer effort of netting, then picking and then shelling them, is a little daunting, and I feel our energies are better used elsewhere. The way to keep your sanity when following principles of sustainability is to know your own limits. So, I am delighted to have used the hazelnuts as a hedging plant, feeling that they fit in beautifully with what we are doing here, but I do not feel compelled to try to use every tiny thing that we produce. I am, however, hoping that the abundance of hazelnuts will act as a decoy crop for the ravenous and destructive cockatoos.

Medlars

This is an old fruit that is planted more as specimen tree than for its fruit, which are brown and need to be 'bletted' before use (this process involves racking them up on straw beds and letting them soften). I then attempt to make jelly out of them. 'Attempt' is the word, as some years it sets, and others it doesn't, leaving me with many jars of syrupy uselessness. When it is a good year and the jelly sets, it is a perfectly brilliant addition to a cheese plate, with a curious but pleasant tannic aftertaste on the back palate.

Peaches

Of all the trees that I want to succeed here, I think it is the peach that I look forward to the most. We have planted two: an Anzac variety, to celebrate my forebears, and a Heritage French variety that has blood-red flesh. Peaches, like many soft fruits, are best enjoyed with minimal intervention: straight from the tree.

Here is my universal fruit chutney recipe, which always tastes like a far-superior bought fruit chutney to me. You can just substitute any fruit for the peaches.

Fruit chutney

MAKES 1.5 KG

2 kg cleaned fruit cut into cm dice

1 tbsp mustard seeds

3 chillies, finely chopped

2 cloves garlic, finely chopped

1 onion, finely chopped

1 piece fresh ginger, 4 cm, finely chopped

600 g brown sugar

220 g sultanas

3 cups white wine vinegar

Combine all ingredients in a large, heavy-based non-reactive stockpot and simmer for about 1 hour or until thickened. Stir gently at regular intervals and take care the mixture does not catch on the bottom of the pot. Spoon into sterilised preserving jars. Seal and store in a cool place away from sunlight. The chutney will keep for at least a year.

Pears

The most elegant of the orchard fruit, pears are such a beautiful shape, and, when ripe, have the most sensual texture. As with the apples, I love their names. Doyenné du Comice, D'Anjou and Conference are three that give me much pleasure.

They are delicious roasted with pork or lamb, and lovely pickled or preserved in a chutney, but are at their best when paired with puff pastry and vanilla ice cream. This recipe includes the poaching instructions for pears but can be a guide for other poached fruit; only the timing may change a little, as it will depend on the size and the ripeness of the fruit that you are using. It also has my foundation salted-caramel sauce recipe that is also great for many dishes.

Pear tart with salted-caramel sauce

1 quantity puff pastry
whipped pouring cream, to serve

For the poached pears
1 kg sugar
1 L water
1 vanilla bean split lengthways and seeds scraped
4 'perfect' pears, peeled

For the salted-caramel sauce
225 g sugar
60 ml water
125 ml pouring cream
60 g unsalted butter, cut into cubes
1½–2 tsp flaked salt or fleur de sel

To make the poached pears, combine the sugar, water and vanilla bean in a large saucepan and bring to the boil, stirring to dissolve the sugar. Reduce to a simmer, then add the pears and gently poach until just cooked. The time will vary, depending on the ripeness and variety of the pears, but start checking with a skewer after about 7 minutes. When cooked, remove the pan from the heat. The pears can be stored in the syrup until you are ready to use them.

For the salted-caramel sauce, combine the sugar and water in a large, heavy-based saucepan and stir over a low heat until the sugar has mostly dissolved. Increase the heat to high and allow the mixture to come to the boil. Use a brush dipped in water to wash down any sugar crystals from the side of the pan, but do not stir the syrup.

As soon as the syrup starts to turn an amber colour, remove from the heat and swirl the caramel around in the saucepan. The caramel will continue to cook and become darker after it has been removed from the heat, but if it does not become a rich amber colour, put the pan back on the heat for 5 seconds, then remove and swirl to mix.

Once it is off the heat, immediately add the cream, whisking constantly. The caramel will rapidly bubble up, but keep whisking until it has stopped bubbling. Add the butter and salt and whisk until the butter has completely melted and is mixed into the caramel. Leave to cool before using, or immediately pour into clean heatproof jars and store in the refrigerator. The sauce will keep for up to a month – it will thicken while chilled, so reheat before using.

When you are ready to assemble the tarts, roll out the pastry to a thickness of about 4 mm. Make yourself a pear-shaped stencil out of stout cardboard – it should be about 1.5 cm bigger than the pears. Cut 8 pear shapes from your pastry and chill while you prepare the pears.

Preheat the oven to 210 °C and line a large baking tray with baking paper.

Carefully remove the pears from the syrup with a slotted spoon and drain on a paper towel.

Cut them in half lengthways and remove the cores. Place the pastry cut-outs on the prepared tray and top each one with a pear half, the cut side down.

Bake for 15 minutes or until the pastry is risen and golden brown. Reduce the temperature to 170 °C and bake for another 10 minutes to cook the pastry through. Remove from the oven.

Serve each tart with a generous helping of salted-caramel sauce and some whipped cream.

Pomegranates

I fell in love with pomegranates when I was kid studying the classics. The myth of Hades abducting Persephone was a favourite. As Persephone sat on the throne in the underworld, eating pomegranate seeds, her mother, Demeter, the harvest goddess, mourned and granted no fertility to the earth. My interest in this myth's explanation of the seasons was a predictor of my future interest in gardening. The diversity of the attachment to pomegranates also fascinated me, as they were representative of love and fertility across all of the Middle East, and used by many religions as such. As an adult cook, I still have a fascination with them; they are little jewels of light that brighten many a Middle Eastern or North African dish I might produce at home. They are perfect added to couscous with raisins and pine nuts, delicious in salads with grilled lamb chops, and a sharp pop of flavour in a watermelon salad.

Prunes

I have spent some time in Agen and its surrounding areas, and I have a deep connection with that part of France. I am always particularly struck by the people's love for and reverence of the plum, which begets the prune. It features in many of the region's specialties and is what distinguishes Armagnac from Cognac.

We have espaliered our D'Agen plums and I have sequestered away a proper French drying rack on which to turn the plums into prunes. When we do produce our own prunes, I suspect I shall put them in a jar, smother them with Armagnac and pull them out for special occasions.

Quinces

This is another of my cherished fruits, and one that is incredibly versatile, especially when you consider it can't be eaten raw. I cook and utilise quinces in numerous ways. For use with cheese and charcuterie, I always pickle a batch, with surprisingly delicious results. I will often braise them with lamb, which works very well in North African–style dishes. For dessert dishes, I will either peel and poach the quinces in basic sugar syrup, leaving them quite a light orange and less sweet, or I will peel and halve them and bake in the oven in sugar syrup, very, very slowly, until they are a deep purple. In the conserving kitchen, I will make paste, jam and jelly from them. These are the many wonders of the quince.

Walnuts

When I look to the south-west from our verandah, I get to see a singular old walnut tree. Walnut trees grow into the most perfect shape. The two that we have planted in the orchard are set to become magnificent specimen trees. I will use the walnuts, but probably mostly as a pickle made from the green nuts.

Buildings

I F YOU ARE lucky enough to buy the part of a subdivided farm that contains all the original buildings, you could be buying a treasure. Or you could be buying yourself demolition tasks and many trips to the tip. Babbington Park came with no fewer than *ten* separate buildings.

Farms are funny things: scatterings of buildings that have popped up as needed, often held together with a bit of welding and a few lashings of binder twine. You can tell a lot about the skills in days gone by from the way sundry farm buildings are constructed. It is clear that Farmer Botheras was very good with a welder and with concrete. Some of his carpentry skills were a little lacking, but he can be forgiven for this because of the sheer scale of his inventiveness.

The house

With so much attention being paid to the garden, the house has been starved for attention in our first years here. A solid Federation building, it has three bedrooms, one bathroom and a separate office. Not a lot of space for four women and many animals to live in, but enough. The house was completely liveable when we moved in, even if we hated the bathroom. It also proved to have an unexpected, but appreciated, shining quality as the months rolled by: it is well insulated and warm. Relying on only wood heating, this is a godsend because, gosh, it gets cold up here.

In the classic country vernacular, the house has a return bullnose verandah. Two sides of it are sealed in with walls and louvres: a space that we refer to as the mudroom, because it's where we take off all our outside clothes and shoes before going inside. It's an absolute must for coats, boots, wet dogs, cat beds, wood stacks and the like. The western side of the house is flanked with windows and doors, and faces out to the beautiful view to the west, taking in the rolling hills, our neighbours' vegetable farm and, of course, our majestic lake. All of this is enjoyed from a broad deck with another bullnose verandah that gives shelter from the summer sun. However, everywhere you look, there are curiosities.

All the verandah posts sit concreted into a metre of agi pipe: an old-fashioned terracotta pipe that was used for drainage. We will never know if they rotted out and were propped up, or maybe the posts were just too short to begin with.

Even more detested than the bathroom was the laundry. It was a hideous tacked-on affair that, apart from being constructed from asbestos sheets, had the worst guttering system in the world. Until it was seen to, with every deluge, poor Susan would have to sweep the water out, cussing and cursing all the while, the ridiculousness of it all heightened by the fact it is 2 metres away from the house well.

We are only just starting to peel back the layers inside the house. The ugly bathroom was dealt with first. And beauty was exposed – the whole room originally had horizontal lining boards, and there were enough to leave to halfway up the walls, and then continue with plaster. Uncovering the bathroom boards led us to discover that the plastered hallway was also concealing beautiful lining boards.

Then we noticed the space between the architrave and the wall was not quite right. Under the thick, old-fashioned plaster of the hallway were duck egg blue lining boards, the paint shining, if a bit cracked, murmuring little stories from long ago.

Next to the bathroom is a full pantry room with funny old wooden shelves. It is like something conjured up from the pages of a 1950s edition of *The Weekly Times*, and a timely reminder that it was important to have a room in which to preserve food and produce. It will be the perfect place to store all our fruit preserved in Fowlers Vacola jars, and all the jams and the chutneys in the years to come, when the orchard is in full swing and other plans have come to fruition.

There are other oddities: the internal doors were not quite right, all being slightly thicker than normal. Again, with a little paint peeling, we discovered all the doors in the house are lovely four-panel doors that have been covered with ply and painted beige.

Tastes and styles change in the life of a 120-year-old house, but I think we will like her best when we have stripped her back to something closer to her original state. With two children on the cusp of adulthood, it seems silly to renovate just yet, though. Both Susan and I feel strongly that, while there must always be room for the children, the house will spend most of its time accommodating two people. And we don't see the need to change it massively; it's fine as it is, so why waste resources turning it into something that it is not?

The church

It sounds very fancy to have a church on your property, but, given that it is Wesleyan, it is more of a plain little chapel than a soaring, vaulted-ceiling spectacular. There was a vigorous push for the Cornish people to immigrate to Australia in the mid-19th century, and the combination of a potato famine and a collapse in the Cornish tin mining industry encouraged many to come. In Cornwall, the people had adopted John Wesley's evangelical revival version of the Protestant faith; he first visited Cornwall in 1743 and made thirty-two subsequent visits. So, by the time Cornish families were emigrating to Australia, the Wesleyan Methodist faith was deeply rooted. It is a show of the strength of the Cornish community here in Lyonville that, in 1887, a block of land opposite the Radio Springs Hotel was purchased and, sometime in the 1890s, a tin and weatherboard chapel was erected to service the local community. Some years later, as both the congregation and local population declined, the little chapel was picked up and moved to the Botheras family's farm, where, for many years, it was just another shed covered in blackberries. Thankfully, the structure held together, including, most importantly, its delightful wood-lined ceiling.

When we acquired Babbington Park, the previous owners had done some renovation work and turned the chapel into a B&B. Before that, the Collings family had used it as a shed and had a carport area as their 'boning room': a place to keep the bandsaw and cut up slaughtered animals used for food. For a moment, Susan and I toyed with the idea of continuing the B&B, but the prospect of online reviews made me shudder. I can just cope with the keyboard warriors attacking the restaurant, but the thought of that level of judgement of our home was too much for me. Oh, how I long for the days of a carefully written complaint letter in the mail, rather than the anonymity of the internet and what it leads to.

We decided that the church would make a great little space for the demonstration cooking classes I would be running. We set about enclosing the carport as a dining area, installing a small AGA stove, and generally tidying and changing the decor. About halfway through the project, another, somewhat unforeseen, complication arose. My mother, Edie, who had been living on her own in suburban Melbourne for twenty-five years, suffered a home invasion, and was not as confident living in her own place as she had been. After much discussion of the pros and cons, it was decided that she would come and live in the church. This sent Susan down a very different track with the renovation, and we proceeded to make the bathroom and doorways much more suitable for an older person. We still do cooking classes in the church, with Edie providing witty commentary from the couch and the odd story about what a naughty child I was.

The shearing shed

There is no doubt in my mind that the shearing shed is both my favourite and the most important building on the property. Nothing else symbolises the struggle, the work ethic and the creative-solution mindset of our forebears more.

The shearing shed is the oldest structure on the property, dated at around 1870. When we arrived, it was in a pretty sad condition, and during our first winter here, the whole south wall fell off in a wild storm.

It is a classic Australian shed, but, with no pictorial evidence of what it looked like originally, we can only piece together through research and common sense what it might have been like when new. Measuring some 18 metres long and 10-and-a-half metres wide, it's a small shed for a small property. It is roughly divided into thirds: one third has a dirt floor and is for hay and feed storages; the other two are in the classic layout of a shearing shed. It has an elevated floor, most of it with grid flooring that allows the excrement and urine to fall through, and a small section with a hard floor. The shed is a two-stand arrangement, allowing two shearers to work at a time. When we inherited it, it had a patchwork of rough corrugated iron hammered to the outside, to try to keep the weather out, and the internal structure was made up of bush poles of various thicknesses. There was a standard pattern of yards and races to allow the flow of sheep, and a concrete pit and trough for pest control, with a run-off down the hill to the Loddon River. The yards were covered by a canopy of blackberries that pushed and poked their way into the structure of the building. The shed looked completely rooted and, to add insult to injury, it was full of debris. On closer inspection,

though, beauty, bushcraft and skill were revealed everywhere. This building represents so much about the conditions of the time when it was built and the changing fortunes of the years to come.

Corrugated iron was certainly proliferating in Australia in the 1870s, but it must be remembered that Lyonville was in timber country and in terrain that was tough to navigate. This was a time when services were orchestrated around a priest moving between churches on horseback, as it was too arduous for a cart. We suspect that the shed was not originally clad in iron. Wood had been harvested in the Wombat State Forest since the 1850s, and a sawmill was in operation from the 1860s almost 'over the road', so we feel that the shed was almost certainly a timber building.

The framework is something to behold: tall, thick, straight trees, stripped of their bark and dropped into the ground; smaller trees laid across as roof trusses. The two long beams are cut from single trees. Each one is roughly squared, the marks of the chopping axe and the broad axe still visible, but not done to perfection. They were possibly cut in haste, as only two sides look attended to with any care. On top of the roof framework lies milled timber: wood cut in lengths about 5 centimetres wide, a feat of work that is in complete contrast to the long beams. On top of that is the remnants of tar paper, and then there is the corrugated iron roof. Much of the construction contributes to the theory that the iron roof came later, and the shed probably had a shingle roof originally.

On the eastern side, which is the shortest side due to the hill it is perched on, we have a face of original slab timber. It is not inconceivable that the whole shed would have been faced in slabs originally. To watch a woodcutter saw slab timber from a green tree is to see a work of both art and craft that I find mesmerising. The sharpness of the axes, the use of a plumb bob, the flick of a string line coated in charcoal. Extraordinary skills are getting lost in the mists of time, simply because there are cheaper, easier ways to do things. The wall dividing the hay area and the sheep area is made from lengths of timber 15 centimetres wide laid in shiplap formation. The floor of the sheep area is panels of intricately worked slats of hardwood, held together with coach bolts; highly worked, and incongruous against some of the more slapdash-looking aspects.

Initially, we had grand plans of turning the shearing shed into a wedding venue. It took a very small amount of time to realise that this would be a distant reality.

Now I should introduce Greg – a friend of Susan's who is an integral part of our lives at Babbington. He is a builder, what we refer to as an 'old-fashioned builder'. He's been doing it for a long time and learned his trade in the years before trusses came preassembled. He is also a man who has had his fill of trying to work with out-of-whack frames and make dilapidated structures sound again. It was with some trepidation that we first asked him to look at the shearing shed. But I recently overheard him talking to a specialist plumber that we had called in to consult on the roof, saying sweetly and lovingly about the shed: 'When I first looked at it, covered in blackberries and full of junk, I thought it was a piece of shit. Having worked on her and with her, I've realised the immense value in her as a historic building that tells so many stories.'

Greg has set to work rebuilding this amazing structure, in the most sensitive way possible. It was discovered that all the round poles were rotten 30 centimetres into the ground, and, of course, there was an incredible lean to the building. We started on the easy end, the northern hay shed side; a less complex part of the structure. We were not in a position to use new round poles, so Greg carefully framed up using square cypress posts, set directly behind the round poles so that you can barely see them. This has the added advantage of creating a squarer canvas to work on. He then removed some of the internal wall and took it to a sawmill to see if he could have hardwood milled to the same specifications; the answer was yes, so timber was ordered. The northern, eastern and western sides of the hay area are now all clad in timber, with sliding wooden doors allowing access to the inside. The interior serves as the night-time lodgings of the cattle, goats and geese. The geese have one side, with six individual pens to allow for breeding-season shenanigans, and the cattle and goats have the other. The cattle have the smaller 'room', and the goats the larger, with pallet beds at various heights for them to play and sleep on.

The shearing side is proving more of a challenge. The southern wall, which fell off in such an inglorious manner, has been remade the same way as the northern wall, but it is the interior that is slowing us down somewhat. With the posts rotting, they have dropped away from roof height and offer no support or integrity to the framework. Some of them are more than half a metre shorter than they should be. Greg has come up with an ingenious solution: he uses a truck jack to jack them up and manages to reblock them, one at a time.

We are at a bit of a standstill now until Susan and I decide what purpose the building is going to fulfil. Will I hold classes in it, will I do events in it? No decisions have been made, but we know now that it won't fall down and we have preserved our own little piece of Lyonville history for another 100 years.

And we finally solved the riddle of the floor. At some stage, it was replaced with panels that came from the cattle cars Victorian Railways used when animals were transported by rail, not by semitrailers. Most older Victorians looking closely at the panels would be reminded of the red rattlers, as there are even remnants of red paint to be found here and there. I imagine the cattle cars must have been going cheap at some point.

Sundry farm sheds

There are three major farm sheds and an assortment of others.

The potato shed

This is the first building you see on entry to the property: a large, rather plain, galvanised iron shed, 26 by 6.5 metres. It has two huge rolling doors on the north face and a funny little set of iron stairs to ascend to floor level. We named it the potato shed, based on its historical use, to distinguish it from the other sheds.

The floor is about a metre off the ground, to enable the loading and unloading of potatoes from both tractors and trucks. It is an incredibly sound shed, supporting the notion that it was professionally built and not just thrown up as the need arose. The most impressive feature of the shed is its floor. This is made of 2.5-centimetre-thick pieces of hardwood. Here and there are bits of damage, from that caused by insects to the odd patch of dampness, but, overall, the floor is yet another reminder that we have landed in a town whose recent history is of timber cutting and milling, and it is a floor that is extraordinary to behold.

The dry nature of the shed has meant that it has become our own personal storage facility. The joining of households in a relatively small house has meant there is a lot to store and sort. Add to that the detritus from fifteen years of restaurants; the 'kit' for outside catering gigs and markets; and, of course, from packing up my mother's house and moving her into the church. Then there are the collections of special 'finds' that may be useful for future renovations (and the round centrepiece as you swing open the doors is my beautiful La Cornue stove, waiting to be installed in the kitchen), and you have a shed that is full to the gunnels. We are lucky to have such a space, and it has made our lives much less stressful, yet I dream often of it being used differently.

The most wonderful use would be as a grown-up bunkhouse and communal living space; it is one of those dreams that is often prefaced with 'If I were rich'. I would engage a clever architect and get them to turn it into a camp for adults. Then I could run a little residential school, where people could experience the joys that are mine, each and every day: the mornings tending to animals, the work in the vegetable garden, the cooking, and all the other delights I get to call my day-to-day existence.

The green shed

Oh my, this is a Farmer Botheras special. The green shed is named for its bizarre painted galvanised iron, in line with the potato shed, just further down the driveway. Measuring 21.5 metres long and nearly 6 metres wide, made up of five bays, and held up by steel pipes inserted into 11-gallon drums filled with concrete, it is an extraordinary feat of homemade building.

The doors are massive welded structures that are extremely heavy, and the floor is dirt. It has power and is a really useful shed. The first bay houses our hay. The second contains seasonal animal enclosures that double as drying racks for shallots, onions and garlic. The third bay stores our firewood; the fourth, the tractor; and the fifth, garden paraphernalia. There are stakes, both metal and wooden; irrigation pipes; and wire fencing by the roll, as we deal in 100-metre rolls. When you are inside this shed, it is obvious that the difference between half a hectare and 10 is scale. The number of things needed to nurture our little farm, and to use everything as responsibly as we can, is staggering. And most things last better if they are put in a shed, away from the elements.

One day we will probably paint this shed, though I suspect I will always call it the green shed. I rather fancy doing something lovely with the door, removing the iron and adding lightweight wooden slats, but we will see.

The brick shed

This too is a phenomenal achievement of do-it-yourself. At the end of the driveway, positioned to be close to the house, is the brick workshop shed. Its distinguishing feature is that it is made of a single skin of brick, defying conventional building techniques. What holds it together so solidly are massive footings of concrete and more steel; quite a lot more steel, really. At 12.5 by 9.5 metres, it is not a small structure either. It is another dirt-floored building with power and a long fixed work bench. It would have been the workshop shed, and we use it to store my old Land Rover, the farm ute and the tip piles and rubbish. It also accommodates the generator that is hooked up to our mains in case of fire or power outages. The bench is now used for far more garden-related than mechanical things, as we need a good sturdy bench to attach our wire bender to, so that we can make all our small gauge pegs and plant supports.

None of these sheds are particularly attractive, but all have elements of charm and wonder. Most importantly, they are all extremely useful. Neither Susan nor I could bear the thought of pulling any of them down and erecting new ones to fulfil the same purpose they already do. To our minds and according to our taste, they have a place in this environment and can be improved with a few decorative flourishes; the criminal waste of resources in actually just pulling them down and starting again, we cannot come at.

One of the curious things about all three sheds, all with massive roofs, is that they have no guttering. This is a peculiarity that will be explained when the subject of our water supplies is explored.

I admit the house's area is somewhat burdened by sheds. As our friend Paul, a landscape designer, has pointed out to us on many occasions, the beauty of the house is completely hidden by the number of ramshackle buildings that hem her in on all sides: a gorgeous turn-of-the-century house, perched high on a windswept hill, cluttered with outbuildings. But the three major sheds all have to stay. They are useful, practical and part of what makes this a farm, as we have never been after a look that is simply one of gracious living.

Next to the brick shed is the garage, a perfectly sweet pitched-roof building. With pleasant proportions and a farm-style look, it is slated to be extended at the back to become the new laundry. As the existing laundry is an excrescence of a boxed fibre cement extension to the back of the house, it really has to go.

Behind the house is a ramshackle building. Housing the outside toilet and a rat-infested storage shed, and extended with bush poles and iron, this shed was great as a temporary goose house when we first arrived, but is being quietly dismantled. It has little or no value to us, and is planted firmly on the northern side of the house. This means that we are not able to see the northern view, which is fast becoming very beautiful, or capture any of the northern light or warmth.

In front of the house to the north are the original chicken coops, which we have mended but will be demolished. To the south is the old milking shed. Again, it is not attractive, and in an awful spot, but both Susan and I have a strange fondness for it. With power and a concrete floor, it is a useful space, but, most importantly, it is the site of the first livestock births on our watch here: Leo and Sunday, twin cashmere goats born to Hazel. For now, it has been fox-proofed for the ducks to live in, but time will tell what becomes of that one.

Buildings need use and upkeep, and it must never be forgotten that the climate in Lyonville is very harsh. The winter is long, the altitude is reasonably high and the winds are battering. I completely understand that someone with a designer's eye can look at our place and want to remove every unsightly building. Taste, style and function are all in the eye of the beholder, and I am a great believer in not pulling down something that is useful. But by removing some of the more unsightly buildings, the view has been opened up and the house feels freer within herself. I have also come to understand why all the buildings were so close to the house. Without the creature comforts we are used to, this would have been a very harsh property to farm and I don't blame Fred for building everything as near as possible.

One last farm building, which is now only a ruin, deserves a mention. The climate in Lyonville has changed dramatically over the past thirty years, but Fred lived here for a very long time before that. North of the old toilet shed is a great deal more concrete; rectangular footings, with the telltale signs of a galvanised ripple sheet set into the concrete – the old glasshouse site. Complete with hardening-off beds on the eastern end, this was where the house vegetables were grown. The glasshouse has long since fallen down; all that remains are the footings. And the furnace shed. The climate meant if you wanted to have more than just root vegetables all winter, you needed a glasshouse that could be heated. Underneath the soil inside the footings is an array of metal pipes that were connected to a basic furnace, so that Fred could raise plants all year round.

The change in both the climate and the water table are canaries in the coalmines for us all. It is sobering to think of the glasshouse that once stood here, a necessity in an era when snow sat on the ground for days in the howling Lyonville winter. So much has altered in this property's lifetime. The markers of change are all around us, if only we care to look.

The new builds

The prospect of new buildings on the property requires very weighted consideration. What is needed, what is useful, what is desirable? It is also a question of priorities: funds need to be allocated to fixing the old, but there is also the desire to create some purpose-built spaces. However, our first two new builds could both be considered follies on my part. As a great lover of English and French garden design of the 18th century, I am rather partial to a folly. Given that we have so many practical sheds, my thinking is that there is always space for a little amusement.

The first building we had constructed was a boathouse. In my last years at Malmsbury, a builder friend of mine constructed a storage shed for my apple and quince crop. It was built over the foundations of the old milking shed, and it was a little like a

scene out of Jasper Conran's *Country*, an evocative photographic journey through rural England. The hardwood boards were radially sawn, giving them a kooky curliness, and they quickly greyed off to look old before their time. I loved that little shed, and somehow it became the representation of all I left behind – the garden, the stones, the trees that I had known since they were spindles precariously defying the weather, and the little rough-sawn shed. So, I asked the same friend to build a little shed down on the lake shore here. Perhaps I thought that if I replicated the Malmsbury shed, the yearning for what I had abandoned would lessen. I was wrong, but each morning, as I look down on that little building, I remember the past fondly and am emboldened to push on with the project at hand.

The boathouse is a delightful little building. It has rough-sawn weatherboards, like its predecessor; and a sweet little pitched roof, which, again, is similar to the Malmsbury shed, but with some flourishes that were missing. It is built on stumps that were once wharf pylons, still with the telltale marks of mussels having grown on them. These old timbers that had been submerged in the sea for decades now find themselves moved and used for dry land footings. On the front is a verandah, for lounging on and gazing across the lake, with huge slabs of timber as steps. The doors are a treasure of the salvage yard: old timber bank-vault doors that were once encased in iron, years of rust staining the timber irrevocably.

The second build seriously fits into the folly category. What is really the new chook house and garden toolshed is disguised as a pigeonnier. I have long been fascinated by the buildings that are stuck in the middle of a paddock, all on their own, and often seen in rural France. This didn't make much sense to me, but once all was explained, I understood perfectly. These buildings were often tall, and had a series of openings and ledges near the top. The insides were generally bare, except for brick or timber work that created a little internal ledge on the inside of all the openings; these were designed for pigeons to roost in. The reason the pigeonniers were out in the middle of fields was that all the poo that collected and dried in the bottom of them was then spread around the adjoining fields as fertiliser. There has always been something very alluring to me about the proportions of these buildings, let alone their quixotic nature. Over the years, I have had many ideas of what my chicken housing should look like, but decided that the pigeonnier model was the way to go.

Instead of it being a hollow building, we have constructed it in two parts, and created a top floor for the poultry and a shed for all the garden hand tools underneath. It truly was as simple as showing Greg a picture of what I wanted, and stepping back and watching him create something incredibly beautiful.

The erecting of these two sheds really highlighted changes in the way people build. While the boathouse is perfectly well constructed, it lacks the finesse of the chook house. The walls are braced with ugly metal strapping (the building-code standard), and the boards were attached with a nail gun, resulting in little rust leaks down the timber as it ages. Metal strapping and nail guns are the norm in building these days, being two of the materials and tools that enable builders to work more efficiently.

Greg took considerable, perhaps old-fashioned, care with his pigeonnier. The building is stick built, with herringbone bracing and a hand-pitched roof. Instead of using radially sawn wood, he used the same rough-sawn hardwood that we have on the shearing shed, and hand-nailed the boards on. The corners are faced with bush poles removed from a shed that we helped to fall down. It is these sorts of things that make a great deal of difference to the overall look of the finished product. The modern quick-and-cheaper methods are not really a replacement for the old skills and crafts that Greg displays in his work. It saddens me that these skills are being lost. The friend who built the boathouse is a terrific craftsman, and, in hindsight, I feel I should have discussed with him all the options of how to proceed with the build, to best showcase both his talents and the final product. In any case, Greg has an innate respect for the buildings on the property, the house and the shearing shed in particular. With any additions that he is responsible for, he wants them to last as long as, and to fit in with, the buildings that are already here.

Buildings, and how we build, are part of the bigger conversation about our sustainability-based life. We want to re-use, repair and restore everything we can. Anything new needs to be built to last for many years, using materials in line with our core values. We are lucky to work with a craftsman who not only has a full toolbox of skills but does things in a way that aligns with our beliefs. This gives us the confidence to ask the right questions and do things once, to last for the long term – and there is nothing more sustainable than that.

Foundational recipes on which to build all good dishes

Everything needs good foundations – buildings, relationships, parenting, farming, living. And cooking is no exception. Some folk in the world of cooking are saying that we have lost the ability to cook the way that our grandmothers and great-grandmothers did. They say we are slaves to recipes; like blinkered horses, following linear instructions but not understanding the fundamentals behind each process.

When you are cooking with produce from your own garden, it is much easier to have an understanding of basic principles, and a good idea of what goes with what, than to search for an individual recipe that might suit your harvest. This is a random selection of recipes that I turn to time and time again.

Basic shortcrust

This can be used in pies, tarts and quiches. Both sweet and savoury, because of the addition of a whole egg, it is also a very well-behaved pastry that doesn't have a tendency to shrink. It's best to rest it in the refrigerator for 20 minutes before rolling. Cook it at between 180 °C and 210 °C, depending on what you are using it in. If you are blind baking a tart case, I would suggest you cook it at the higher temperature, but with a frangipane tart or a filled pie, I would cook it at 180 °C.

125 g butter
210 g plain flour
a pinch of salt
1 egg
25 ml cold water

You can make this pastry on a benchtop by hand, in a bowl by hand, in a stand mixer with the paddle attachment or in a food processor.

Chop the butter into small cubes. Work it through the flour and salt until it resembles coarse breadcrumbs.

Make a well, add the egg and water, and bring together into a dough.

Basic quiche filling

This can be used with a variety of flavours: leek and Gruyère, onion and bacon, roasted tomato and feta, spinach and mushroom. I always like to blind bake my quiche pastry to golden brown first.

3 egg yolks
1 whole egg
300 ml thickened cream
salt and pepper

Whisk all ingredients together. When it comes to seasoning, be mindful of the filling you are using: for example, if the feta is quite salty, then you won't need as much salt. Pour into the pre-baked crust in the quiche tin and cook at 160 °C until it has just set. How long this takes will depend on the size and the depth of the quiche. If you are using a flan tin that is 1.5 cm high, it will take about 45 minutes. If you are making a classic deep quiche (5 cm deep), it will take almost 1½ hours.

Basic thickened sauce

A roux is usually equal amounts of fat (often butter) and flour cooked together, with a hot liquid added gradually. The more liquid is added, the thinner the roux becomes. This is the basis for bechamel, and for such dishes as cream of chicken soup, where you start with a roux and then add chicken stock. The below method is also used for soufflé bases, with a smaller liquid-to-roux ratio; and for croquettes, using even less liquid.

50 g butter
50 g plain flour
500–1000 ml stock or milk, hot
salt and pepper

In a heavy-bottomed saucepan, melt the butter over medium heat. Add the flour and stir vigorously; add the hot liquid a little at a time until you reach the desired consistency, stirring all the while. Season to taste, and use.

Basic braising technique

Braising is one of the best ways to cook secondary cuts of meat. Essentially, it is the process of taking a piece of meat – usually larger ones, rather than meat dices – sealing it and then placing it in an oven dish. The meat is then semi-submerged in stock and covered, and placed in a slow oven for some hours, depending on the size. This process changes the tough sinew and cartilage into gelatine, thus rendering the final product tender and unctuous.

This is a recipe that can be used with beef, lamb or pork cuts. Instead of the red wine, a combination of wine and stock can be used. In fact, beer, or beer and stock, can also be used to great effect. The tomatoes and tomato paste don't have to be used either; it all depends on personal taste.

If you want more vegetables, add diced potatoes or blanched baby potatoes and baby carrots when the meat is in its final thirty minutes of cooking.

Braised meat

SERVES 6

1.5 kg untrimmed flat-cut brisket or piece of neck or chuck steak

salt and freshly ground pepper

2 tbsp grape seed oil

2 large onions, diced

3 celery stalks, diced

2 carrots, diced

5 garlic cloves, smashed

750-ml bottle full-bodied red wine

6 sprigs thyme

2 bay leaves

1 can whole peeled tomatoes

1 tbsp tomato paste

Preheat the oven to 160 °C. Season the meat with salt and pepper. Heat the oil in a large ovenproof pot at a medium-high temperature. Seal the brisket, turning occasionally, until browned all over (8–10 minutes); transfer to a plate. Pour off the fat from the pot; discard. Add a little more oil to the pan, place the onions, celery, carrots and garlic in the oil and sauté for 5–10 minutes.

Remove from the pan, add the wine to the pot and bring to the boil; add thyme, bay leaves, tomatoes, tomato paste, and stir to combine; season with a little salt and pepper. Place the vegetables in the wine and then the meat on top of the vegetables. Cover and braise in the oven, spooning juices, onions and tomatoes over the brisket every 30 minutes, until the meat is fork-tender (4–5 hours). Uncover the pot; place the meat back in the oven till it is browned and the sauce has thickened (about 30 minutes). Skim the fat from the surface of the sauce; discard. Remove the meat from the pot, and slice against the grain to serve.

If you are not serving it immediately, transfer the meat to a large bowl and strain the braising liquid into a separate container. Cover and chill for at least 4 hours and up to 4 days. To serve, preheat the oven to 160 °C. Skim the fat from the surface of the sauce; discard. Cover and reheat the brisket in the sauce for 1–1½ hours.

Basic emulsified sauce

The emulsified sauce family generally covers mayonnaise and hollandaise, even though a shaken dressing could also be considered an emulsified sauce. The below process involves using egg yolks to bind acid and fat. In mayonnaise styles, raw egg yolk is used with acid and oil; in the hollandaise and béarnaise variants, a sabayon is made with the yolks and the acid, and then clarified butter is added. I use these basic recipes, but have a tendency to tinker with the amount of acid, depending on what the final use of the sauce is; and the amount of fat, depending on the final consistency you are looking for, as more fat will make it thicker.

Mayonnaise

2 egg yolks
2 tsp Dijon mustard
a good pinch of salt
300 ml grape seed oil
1–3 tsp lemon juice or vinegar

Whisk the yolks and the mustard together with the good pinch of salt. Add the oil slowly – a few drops at a time at first – whisking all the while. Once the emulsion seems stable, you can increase the flow. After putting in the oil, add the acid to taste. Correct the seasoning with more salt, if required; and a little pepper, if desired.

Hollandaise

4 egg yolks
300 g unsalted butter, melted and warm
20 ml lemon juice
salt and pepper

Find a heatproof bowl that fits neatly over a wider saucepan. Half fill the saucepan with water and bring to a simmer. Place the yolks in the bowl with 2 tbsp of warm water. Place the bowl over the saucepan and whisk for a couple of minutes until you have a light sabayon. Remove the bowl and place onto a bench, and start to whisk in the butter, very slowly at first. Once the emulsion has been established, you can increase the flow. Avoid using the milk solids and liquids at the bottom of the melted butter. Whisk in the lemon juice, and season with salt and pepper. If the sauce is too thick for your liking, it can be thinned with a splash of hot water.

Two must-haves

Custard is an easy way to dress up many desserts. It can be made with milk, for a thin pouring custard; thickened cream, for a thicker custard; or with pure cream. Once refrigerated, milk custard will remain a pouring consistency, thickened cream custard will be a thick pouring consistency, and pure cream custard will set solid. Custard can take on many flavours. Infusion is the most common way of adding flavour, with vanilla bean, or lemon or orange rind. You could use roasted nuts that are then strained out, and a variety of spices work well. Or flavours can be added at the end: a little handful of dark chocolate callets, or a slosh of alcohol. And everyone needs a good pancake mix in their repertoire.

Basic custard

500 ml milk or cream
125 g caster sugar
6 egg yolks

In a heavy-based saucepan, bring the milk/cream to scalding point. In a bowl, whisk the yolks and the sugar together. Pour the scalded dairy over the yolks, whisking all the while. Rinse out the saucepan, place the mix back into it, and cook over medium heat, stirring all the while with a wooden spoon. Cook until the custard coats the back of a spoon. Egg yolks will curdle between 80 °C and 84 °C, so caution is needed.

Strain into a jug.

If you are infusing flavour, add the item, e.g. orange rind, to the milk or cream first, bring to scalding point and allow to sit for at least 10 minutes before you proceed with making the custard.

Basic pancake mix

1 cup plain flour
1 tsp sugar
1 tsp baking powder
1 egg
1 cup milk
pinch of salt

Place the dry ingredients in a bowl and mix together. Make a well in the centre, add the egg and then the milk, and whisk together to a smooth batter. It cooks best in clarified butter. I like to eat my pancakes with whipped cream and maple syrup, but in berry season, they are delicious topped with a slightly warmed compote of berries and pure cream.

Water

WATER – IT'S THE gold of the 21st century.

When you move away from access to town water, your whole concept of water changes. Town water – water that is plumbed directly to your house from reservoirs – seems endless. In times of drought, many people are alerted on the nightly weather report to water being in diminishing supply, but in times of plenty, not much thought is given to it.

I have learned much about water in my time in the country: how it is used, how it is wasted and how not understanding its finite nature can threaten to destabilise entire communities. If you live in town, you only have to conduct a little experiment for half an hour to get an idea of what it is like to rely on tanks and pumps. If you go outside and turn your water off at the mains, and then go back inside, in that half hour I am sure someone in the house would like to go to the toilet, do the dishes, boil a kettle or put some washing on – and Murphy's law would probably ensure that all four were happening at once.

But imagine what it would be like if you turned the tap on and there was no water available. This is what it is like in the country if you run your tank dry, or your pump dies. It's not fun, but it can teach you some very sensible habits that will mean little water is wasted and you get the most out of every litre.

At Babbington Park, we have plenty of water. It comes from the sky and comes from deep beneath the soil; the history of water here is fascinating and its complexities many. There is always a part of my mind that is thinking about, and working on, water. Perhaps we should all adopt this state of mind: a constant awareness and vigilance regarding where water is coming from, where it is going and how much is wasted.

The 'lake' is one of the most beautiful features of the property. Susan refers to it as a lake on the grounds that it is spring fed, large and picturesque. She often reminds me that a dam is a muddy hole filled with water from the sky, whereas our body of water is filled from the underground springs. It is artificial; dug originally, we believe, and expanded later. From the western face of our house, the ground slopes away down to the gully, and the lake sits at the foot of the hill and is a highlight of the view from our house's wide verandah. The western edge of the lake is crowned with gum trees, which create an optical illusion. The lake is very deep on its western side, some 14 metres, and the walls fall sharply to the beginnings of the Loddon River. The trees look as if they are a regular height, yet when you are in the gully, you realise they are massive trees. On the southern side of the lake, there is a cleverly constructed overflow, complete with a grate to stop trout (which were held there long ago) from escaping. At the northern end, springs run in a perpetual stream, keeping the lake full to the brim. The overflow feeds the Loddon, and in gorse- and blackberry-removal work, we have discovered another spring that runs from under the north-west side of the hill and also trickles into the Loddon.

Cutting a swathe down the hill and through the bottom paddock is the line of springs. This is no winter creek – these are seven separate springs, finding their way from deep underground and all converging in a single line at the surface. In our first year here, we noticed that the sloping paddock to the north of the springs was always green, giving us a greater understanding of which direction the water was coming from. It has been massively important to us to watch and learn from the subtle changes that happen over the acreage across a twelve-month period.

In our first six months, I bought a very smart go-anywhere lawn mower. Before we stocked the land with animals, I spent an enormous amount of time mowing. While many might think this was a bit of a waste of time, I found it extraordinarily constructive. I learned about where wet spots were, how grass grew in different areas and had a physical link with, and understanding of, the undulation of the land. To traverse each and every metre of ground on a mower enables you to feel the land, as opposed to just siting it. I also gained more perspective on the property, as I could view the land from positions and angles that are not seen on our well-worn paths: what the house looks like from the bottom paddock where the sight lines disappear, where might be a good place for a line of trees. There is nothing like mowing to bring you up close and personal with every metre of your property, and time helps you understand the nuances of the home that you have bought.

Like many things here, the run of springs needs much restoration work. It is full of weeds and rushes, choked with mud and silt, and it is a delicate operation to clean up years of neglect. It is important to regularly remove non-indigenous vegetation and excess silt from the springs, as they interrupt the flow and can affect the quality of the water. The springs can be easily damaged and it is not advisable to use heavy machinery. Much care needs to be taken with levels, so that the point at which the water comes from the earth is not changed in any way.

Initially, I tried to clean the springs out manually, with fire and brute force; standing knee deep in mud and water, hauling out clumps of reeds by hand. This was vicious work that often saw me upended, with the reeds scoring points against me as I struggled to remove myself from the 'drink'. I didn't remove enough of the reeds and weeds on my first attempt, and, in the months that followed, any victory I had was soon forgotten as they grew back. The winter of

2020 saw a different weapon enlisted: a new tractor with a small back-hoe attachment. It is something that I can sit on and use to quietly, quietly remove all the reeds and weeds, while being very conscious of where each of the sister springs rise, so that they can join with each other, sing the song of creation and celebrate what they bring.

We feel the responsibility of having a special water source and have learned to respect its inherent fragility. There is a faint possibility that when we arrived here and if we had had the funds, we would have attempted to clean and sculpt the spring line with big earthmoving equipment. Knowing what we know now, this would probably have destroyed that water source, by crushing the careful network of cracks and fissures that allows the water to come from underground. As it is, our patience and painstaking approach to the rejuvenation work should be rewarded in the years to come, with a healthier and more dynamic stream.

Having a spring-fed lake means we don't struggle with the loss of water to evaporation. But evaporation is one of the key factors for farmers trying to maintain water stocks, as large bodies of water lose an enormous amount in rainless summers, with the water just disappearing into the atmosphere. The fate of open irrigation channels and aqueducts is much the same. As the climate changes, much of this technology has become outdated and outmoded, while our systems can be more naturally regenerative, as our water comes from underground. But underground water is equally precious – we all need to learn how to use water better, particularly that from beneath the earth.

At Babbington, we have studied the methods of farmer and conservationist Peter Andrews and his practices in rehabilitating water-deprived landscapes. When we noticed that the paddock to the north of the springs was much greener than that to the south, we took affirmative action. Ten metres off the mouth of the spring, we constructed a crude damming device, out of a couple of star pickets and some sturdy large timbers. The dam doesn't stop the flow of water, it just slows it – and the result? The green patch on the southern side of the springs increased from 5 metres to over 50 metres in a twelve-month period. Not only does this help with the growth of our grass and pasture, but it has a wonderful effect on the health of the soil and subsoil. All that dirt will be teeming with microscopic organisms, having been given a new lease on life with just one simple adjustment.

Behind the house, we have a well. It still has a sad-looking dog kennel tilted back from the pump that we inherited; pumps need covers, and old dog kennels can do the trick. I had a well in Malmsbury, 2 metres of which was faced beautifully in bluestone. The one in Lyonville is much more utilitarian – no fancy stonework here. It's a deep well, being some 13 metres. When I peer into the darkness, I can only see a glimmer of water. It is a tease; you know it is there but you desperately want it to climb the walls to meet your eyes. In three years, I have only seen a glint and a glimmer many metres down.

The well is covered by rough concrete, with sawn-off metal struts. They tell a story of the great Australian farm pump: the windmill. The windmill is long gone, and in its place is an ugly aqua pressure pump, half covered by the equally unromantic kennel. It amazes me how the workings of a farm always took precedence over beauty and comfort. I cannot imagine how intrusive the noise from the windmill would have been that close to the house. Before an indoor toilet was installed, you would have had to duck out to the back privy, past the windmill, in all weather. I would love to have a windmill replace the pressure pump, but Susan's not too keen on its sound next to the house. But wind turbines and pumps are coming along in leaps and bounds, and I have no doubt that, before our time at Babbington is done, we will have wind-driven water and power. Sometimes it is better to bide one's time and put up with what you have, knowing there is a better solution in development.

Lyonville has an average yearly rainfall of over 1100 millimetres, and potatoes, the traditional crop of the area, have a voracious appetite for water. That magical invention the windmill would rhythmically pull that water up and deposit it into a tank. In Farmer Botheras's time, there was a large oval tank on a stand in the backyard. Up until the early 1990s, that system managed to provide two houses with water and irrigate 30-plus hectares of land. The Collings family report that around the time there was an upheaval in the district, with transitions from farming to lifestyle properties, the increase in tourism and bottled water, and every new land holder's propensity to sink a bore, the well failed to keep up. Since the early 1990s, the demography and the council zoning of the area has changed considerably; our land is classified as 'Rural Living'. With these changes, the water table has dropped further. We can use the well for eight to nine months of the year, but over the peak summer months, it is dry. Perhaps it is a blessing that the windmill is gone – the song that she would sing on a summer's night would be all the more pitiful knowing that she was barren and all that labour would be in vain.

There are many things that we can do to interrupt the draining of the aquifers. Everyone needs to think about their need for water before starting an enterprise on the land, no matter how big or small. There are many properties around us that have part-time occupants who have sunk bores and have automatic watering systems. There are other ways of growing gardens: make sure you have adequate tanks, research which plants thrive in your area and are quite hardy. Too, understand your weather conditions and think about others in your community. Are there farmers near you? Do they need the water for food production? Do you have water-efficient house and garden design? Do you mulch efficiently prior to the summer, to conserve water? Asking such basic questions can make a difference to everyone and everything around you. And many of these considerations should also be taken into account if you live in the city; the more carefully you use water both inside and out, the less is being drained from finite sources.

When the well ran dry, the Collings family had an ingenious solution, installing a concrete tank in the backyard with a curious pump. When we bought the property, the tank made no sense to us. There seemed to be nothing going into it, but an irrigation pipe came out the bottom that we traced to all the stock troughs on the property that were fitted with float valves. When we finally met Daniel Collings, who had grown up on the farm, he showed Susan how it worked.

They had put in a very low-tech pump called a ram pump. David took Susan all the way to the creek below the dam. There, in not so excellent condition, given that a tree had fallen on it, was the remnants of the ram pump. The system – a pump that uses no power and manages to pump water hundreds of metres up a steep hill to fill the concrete tank – is as simple as it is miraculous. It works on water displacement theory. A 5-centimetre pipe comes out from the lake and down the steep incline, into a horizontal pipe that is fitted with two valves, a hammer and an upright pressure pipe. Coming from the upright pressure pipe is a 2-centimetre pipe that runs all the way back up the hill. As the water comes gushing in, it goes through a valve that only opens one way; the water is forced down to the hammer; on the down stroke of the hammer, the water is forced into the upright pipe, where it cannot escape because of a one-way valve. With each stroke of the hammer, the pressure builds until it is safe to turn the tap to allow the water to escape through the 2-centimetre outlet and make its way up the hill to the storage tank.

Apart from the sheer wonder that this pump invokes in me, it seems a deeply environmentally friendly unit. It uses no power

RECIPE FOR A KINDER LIFE

except for the hydropower involved, and it shares the water equally between the farmer and the river system. When you listen to it operating, it is as if it is singing, 'One for me, one for the river, one for me, one for the river ...' When I think about our inherited reliance on power and petrol to drive our water, it is comforting to think that only thirty years ago, a lot of that work was done with much more sustainable methods. This is something that I hope we can revert to.

Our main use of water is in the vegetable garden and orchard. The decorative garden has been carefully planned so that it uses the least amount of water possible. The orchard will use more water in its early years but, as it matures, its needs will modify. At present, we run big trigger-head sprinklers over the area a couple of times a week in the drier months, and water each tree individually once a fortnight when it is really dry and hot. As we do this with a water cube pulled behind the tractor or a ute, we often take the opportunity to add our weed tea to the cube to feed the trees at the same time. Once the trees are established, they will become a little less sensitive and needy. They will develop a shade canopy and leaf mass that will both collect water and prevent some of the evaporation.

Mulching is vastly important in the early years, protecting a small and vulnerable root mass. We often lay chicken wire around the trees, to discourage chickens scratching and exposing the roots. Like weeding and mowing, this can be problematic at times, but it will help to give the trees the best chance of thriving despite the various obstacles that we throw at them.

The trees are planted so that, in full growth, there will not be a lot of space in between them, creating a soft green microclimate. This is also one of the aims for the hedgerow that surrounds the orchard: it will create a sturdy, but interesting, windbreak and contribute to a softer microclimate inside the orchard.

186

The vegetables are a little different. The situation in the first years will be much harder than in five or ten years' time, as, until the orchard and the hedge of hazelnuts planted around the vegetable area grow, the microclimate is very harsh. At the top of a hill, the wind is very drying, no matter what direction it comes from. So we have installed a fairly straightforward eight-zone irrigation system. This allows us twelve outlets, plus the poly tunnel, to be controlled by timers. Each of those outlets has a standard click-on head so that we can vary what we attach to it: sometimes it may be drip hoses, sometimes trigger-head sprinklers, sometimes wobble-head sprinklers. Our decisions are based on what sort of plants or seeds are in the ground and what their individual needs are. The ability to chop and change has been very necessary, as we have found that not one system suits all the permutations and combinations of our plot. Too, we try to use as little water as possible and strive to use it as effectively as possible. The wind is often a determining factor for what sort of irrigation we use in the vegetable garden, as there is little point in using a trigger head if it is only going to be blown off course. In saying all this, I hope that when the hedging has grown up to protect the vegetable plots, we will be able to move to a more stable set-up.

The change in the property's water fortunes explains that other peculiarity: none of the sheds have gutters. The church has been renovated to include gutters, and the house has a clumsy retrofit guttering system that is odd, to say the least. There is a large poly tank next to the church, and a large poly tank next to the house, in the absolute worst position. It appears that, due to the historical abundance of water, there was no need to collect any from the buildings. How times have changed.

The vexed issue of water rights has also complicated things. There is only so much water that we can draw from the lake for domestic and stock purposes. Water for the vegetable garden needs to be collected or bought. We are working with a plumber to devise a master plan for the water collection on the property. This will mean guttering all existing buildings, installing a tank that holds 200,000-plus litres of water, removing the ugly tanks, laying hundreds of metres of pipe, and investing in pumps that can send water hither and yon. The quote is eye watering, at close to six figures, and this is the scale of work that is never done in a residential-size property. With our stock, the vegetable garden, the domestic garden and two residences, it is imperative to me to do it once and get it right. Water is the absolute lifeblood of all that we do here.

While we can sit on the deck of the boathouse on a languid afternoon, looking out across a body of water and thinking how lucky we are, there is something a little disquieting about knowing the intricacies and costs of actually using that water. In working through our complex water needs, I am always astounded by how much we require and how much water we could collect. 'Water maths', as I call it, is important for everyone. To work out how much water you can collect from a roof, you multiply the square metres of your roof by your average rainfall in millimetres. If we gutter all three of our big sheds, we could collect over 450,000 litres of water. When I transpose that to the vegetable garden's needs, it equates to only forty-five days of watering. It just doesn't seem very much.

When thinking about urban dwellers who wish to collect their own water for their garden, the solution is not always as simple as 'Let's put in a tank!' I think that many people would be astounded, and a little disappointed, to realise how quickly a full tank of water can be used. The average flow rate of a standard garden hose is about 37.5 litres per minute, or 2250 litres per hour. An average slimline tank holds just over 2000 litres, so just running the sprinkler for an hour can drain it.

It is important to me to make my garden as water efficient as I possibly can. Having Mum living here illustrates the point perfectly. During her years in the city, she was vexed some summers when there were water restrictions. This was nothing to the irritation she felt here the first time she realised that she had actually run out of water, and that her tank was empty. She is now a great deal more careful with how she uses water but also splashes out and buys tank loads in the summer, thinking that because her garden gives her so much pleasure, it is worth the expense. As she is well into her eighties, I am loath to rain on her parade and suggest that there might be some more sensible plants she could grow that guzzle less water than her prized roses.

The second summer we were here, the main pump to the vegetable garden broke. It was in a period where it didn't rain for fifteen weeks, and we bore huge losses: row upon row of vegetables perished within a four-day period. Our dependence on machinery and our lack of skills in finding where the fault was had terrible consequences that year, but Susan and I learned a valuable lesson and have both acquired thorough knowledge of pumps and plumbing fittings. Water is the most precious resource we have. It is all around us in so many forms here at Babbington; yet, if one domino falls, the whole lot can come cascading down.

Probably our most important use for water is fire safety. Being in close proximity to the Wombat State Forest, we are in a high-risk area come fire season. All house tanks are kept full in the summer. There is a green belt kept around the houses, and fire sprinklers on the roofs. The green belt consists of lawn and garden areas that are kept watered and lush, so that they act as a non-combustible barrier protecting the buildings if a fire were to roar through. A generator has been installed, so that we are able to operate pumps and fire hoses if the dark day comes that the power goes out. There are far more glamorous ways to spend money, but sound investment in the infrastructure of water is, to my mind, imperative. I know the pain of losing plants to broken pumps and lack of water; I cannot even imagine the pain of watching all the assets and work go up in flames.

The simplicity and beauty of water is never lost on me. Most of the time, she is singing to me. There is the bubbling of the springs, the gurgling of the stream that those springs become; the click, click, whir of the impact sprinklers; the spin of the wobble-head sprinklers; the gushing of the newly redirected gutters into the well. They are sounds of happiness and prosperity. And there is the silent water, which is collected by our enormous manna gum. As we often sit below the cloud line here at Babbington Park, she dutifully gathers all that she needs. I marvel at the eucalypt's ability to collect moisture on the leaves that then drips into pools beneath her. On many a morning when there has been absolutely no rain overnight, the geese and ducks are delighted to play in the puddles under the gum.

Recipes for the water-based fundamentals

I have spent some time cooking in a commercial kitchen that uses tank water only. It makes you realise how much water you use in a kitchen – be it for washing vegetables, cooking stock, boiling pasta or just plain old dishwashing. Without water, we cannot grow food and we cannot cook many foods. Many fundamental things completely revolve around water. One of the most fundamental things in my kitchen is the making of stocks. These stocks go on to become liquids that I braise and stew in, soups, and sauces that finish dishes.

'Saucier' can be translated into English as 'sauce cook'. As well as making sauces, the saucier makes stews and hot hors d'oeuvres, and sautés food to order. The literal translation of what a saucier is gives many clues to the position of stocks and sauces in a kitchen, and where they lead. A general overview of the continuum tends to go stocks, broths, stews: stocks being the liquid, broths being the liquid with benefits, and stews being the 'benefits', with the liquid more evaporated. Stocks are the foundation of so many cooking and saucing techniques used in the modern kitchen, including my own. I would heartily recommend that everyone have a decent 10- to 15-litre stockpot at home.

Below are recipes for some essential liquids that, of course, all come back to water. (When I refer to 'mirepoix', this is the kitchen term for the stock vegetables and aromatics.)

Chicken stock

2 kg chicken bones
2 carrots
2 onions
4 sticks celery
1 bay leaf
thyme
parsley stalks
leek tops
water

Place bones in a 7.5–10 L stockpot, cover with cold water and bring to the boil.

Skim. Add mirepoix. Simmer for 4 hours, skimming occasionally. Strain.

Veal stock

5 kg veal bones
3 carrots
4 onions
½ bunch celery

1 bay leaf

2 sprigs thyme

a few parsley stalks/leek tops (optional)

water

Place bones in a 20–25 L stockpot, cover with cold water and bring to the boil.

Skim. Add mirepoix. Simmer for 8 hours, skimming occasionally. Strain.

Sugar syrup

A basic sugar syrup for poaching fruit is made with one part water and one part sugar. Just bring the two to the boil together, and add your aromatics of choice.

Cordials

Homemade cordials are a great way to use up fruit that is less than perfect. And you can adjust the quantities in the recipe according to your random quantities of harvest.

Rhubarb and ginger cordial

1 kg rhubarb

100 ml water

2.5-cm piece of ginger

500 g raw sugar per 1 L liquid

Trim the rhubarb and chop into 10-cm pieces. Place this in a large saucepan and add the water. Grate the ginger into the mix. Bring to the boil and simmer until the rhubarb has collapsed. Strain through a sieve and measure. For every litre of liquid, weigh out 500 g raw sugar.

Combine the strained liquid and sugar in a saucepan and bring slowly to the boil, then boil for a couple of minutes. Check the taste; if you have a sweet tooth, you might like to add a little more sugar. Bottle and refrigerate.

Blackcurrant cordial

300 g raw sugar
300 ml water
zest and juice of 2 lemons
450 g blackcurrants

Place the sugar and water in a saucepan, and slowly bring to the boil. Once the sugar has dissolved and the syrup boiled, add the lemon juice and zest, and the currants. Cook until the currants have softened or burst. Strain through a fine sieve and keep in the fridge.

Creatures

WHEN I FIRST met Susan, it was my geese, not me, that caught her eye. For many years, I identified as a poultry fancier and had kept a small flock of Sebastopol geese. They are famous for their split-feather gene, which gives them glorious, fluffy petticoats when they're in full plumage, and makes them look like they have been dragged through a hedge backwards when they're moulting. Susan, it transpired, had always wanted some Sebastopols. I am sure I was just part of the package, giving a curious new meaning to the expression 'chick magnet'. Along with my Sebastopols, I ran several pens of rare-breed chickens, which she wasn't so enamoured with. When I moved to Babbington, all the geese and the chickens came with me, like a funny old dowry.

Having lived at Malmsbury for many years, I had my pens and grazing routines for my poultry very well sorted. One of our first building exercises when we arrived in Lyonville was to shore up a fairly ramshackle and obviously not fox-proof chicken house. It had good bones, though, with a concrete floor and sturdy hardwood structure. To accommodate my various breeds of chickens and to prevent the roosters from fighting and crossbreeding, the building needed to be divided into four rooms.

We initially used a couple of rolls of electric netting fence, and when we realised that the chickens would be there for a while, we invested in the wonderful Eucifence, from Wattle & Wire on the Victorian coast. This fencing material comes in 10-metre rolls and is constructed in the same way as traditional French and English chestnut paling fence. It is made from a hardy eucalypt precision cut and held together with corrosion-resistant wire. It has proved marvellously successful and, while it is still in its temporary position, we will be able to roll it up and re-use it when it has a permanent home.

Because our chickens have a rotational outside roster, we give them a lot of TLC in their locked-up days. Morning and night, they get a helping of grain, and those that are not grazing get greens from the garden. Often, we will tie up bunches of mixed greens or a whole spent or not-quite-right cauliflower or cabbage. The chickens get lots of extra exercise jumping up and pecking at them, and it helps to keep the floor of the coop clean. Each summer, the local farmer comes and cuts 400-odd bales from two of our paddocks, and these are stored for winter feeding and bedding for the rest of the year. The pens are lined with hay and regularly cleaned out, with the spent bedding layered in our compost heaps.

The main predators of our chickens are foxes, and, due to diligent lock-up and let-out practices, we have created a different problem for ourselves – one that many people don't get to experience: the chickens get quite elderly and stop laying. Neither of us has much truck with the concept of killing them off when they are no longer laying, so we have a coop filled with happy ageing chickens. They are living their best life, but not giving much back: with an average life span of eight years, they eat far more in grain than they provide in eggs. When they finally fall off the perch, they are buried deep in the compost, to become part of the regenerative cycle.

The geese gave rise to pressing issues when they were moved. At that stage, I had only three geese left, as my main flock had succumbed to an unknown disease. There was the old girl, at least twelve; her daughter, ten; and the gander, also pushing twelve. Geese also need fox-proof lodgings at night and our eyes quickly turned to a shed near the house, where they would remain until their superior lodgings were built eighteen months later. This shed was an extension of the old outhouse building, where the ubiquitous outside dunny resides. The previous owners had used it as a wood-storage area. After a fair amount of clearing-up, we were left with reasonable floor space, but a slightly rickety structure of bush poles and galvanised iron. It was decided that it would do in the short term. Firm doors and stout wire were fitted, and the geese were safe from overnight predators and able to roam the farm during the day.

Then, as soon as Susan had the space, she decided to embark on some goose ownership of her own. Off she popped in the ute, and came home with nine new Sebastopols for herself and a goodwill gesture of a pair of Toulouse geese for me. This was fine, it was winter, but I knew what was coming. Ganders make a lot of noise in spring, and sure enough, when it came, the noise and the activity levels ramped up. The short-term goose accommodation needed some serious attention, with us having to cordon off the couples so the ganders didn't fight all night. While I was working at the restaurant each day, Susan was furiously assembling 'bedrooms' for the geese, lashing old pallets together with cable ties. She felt that each new couple needed the privacy of their own bedroom, and protection from each other.

While it may sound odd, geese are wonderful creatures to keep. They work very closely with the cycles of the sun, waking at the same point just after sunrise each morning and coming in for bed at the same point just before dark each night. And they form strong bonds with their partners and offspring, always preferring to be housed with their immediate family at night. Geese can live for twenty-five years, so they are not a bird to take in on a whim: you need to be prepared to commit to them for the long term. And don't believe anybody who tells you they mate for life! They certainly like to be put to bed with their mate each night, but on a spring day, if another gander is not looking, all the ladies are fair game.

Eighteen months in the old shed was a serious trial. The roof leaked, and the walls would come away in strong winds, so my tiny partner would scale a ladder, no matter the weather, and lash one pole to another with more cable ties. Understandably, for so many reasons, new lodgings became a priority, and the geese now live happily in the restored end of the shearing shed, with separate pens, hanging facilities for their water buckets, and a clean-out roster that would put a Melbourne Cup–winning stable to shame.

Geese are very messy creatures, so their bedding is another nutrient-rich source for our compost heaps. They are also very greedy birds: four geese can eat the same amount of grass in a day as one sheep. They are efficient grazers, with their beaks containing rows of serrated teeth that strike fear into many, as they have a reputation for chasing and catching the upper inner thigh.

The geese are only kept as part of our breeding program so as to sustain a rare breed; Susan has been a vegetarian for many years. It was decided when we moved to Babbington that we would keep no creatures for culling. At the end of each breeding season, she finds homes for all the geese she doesn't want to hang on to.

We have lost a couple of geese over the years. On one particularly sad day, they all came running up the hill early, for us to discover at lock-up time that my old gander was missing. He had been felled by a fox in the bottom paddock. We have since become very sensitive to their movements and are always on the lookout for foxes and eagles. One of the indelible lessons we have learned keeping animals and poultry is that danger and mishap are always at hand, and it is imperative that someone is always home. Even with these precautions, last spring we lost a fully feathered gosling to a family of eagles.

To celebrate our fiftieth birthdays, Susan and I went on a little jaunt to Italy, on a holiday conceived and booked some time before the idea of Babbington Park became a reality. I thought it would be terribly romantic to stay in a restored stone farmhouse in Tuscany, on a sustainable cashmere goat farm. It was delightfully romantic, except that in the mornings, I overly enjoyed spending time with the owner, an expat American called Nora, helping her with chores around the farm. Very quickly a routine of farm jobs in the morning and tourism in the afternoon was agreed on; otherwise, I might have seen nothing of Tuscany. It was here that we observed, up close and personal, the keeping of cashmere goats.

Nora explained that her decision to start a herd of cashmere goats came about because she wanted to raise an animal that could provide an income without being slaughtered, was a good mother and was intelligent. This matched our desire not to keep animals that were destined for the meat market. But it is important to note that the textile industry is racked with as many non-sustainable practices as is the food chain. As goods like cashmere become more and more in demand, and cheaper and cheaper, the quality of the herds and the animal husbandry suffers. Nora works tirelessly with an international body to try to keep the quality and production of cashmere protected.

When Susan and I returned to Australia, we promptly found ourselves a cashmere breeder and bought six goats from Queensland – four young does and two does in kid – and had them transported down. As soon as they were released from the float, I knew I was in trouble.

Even though I have kept goats in the past, I had given no thought to the fact that they jump and climb. Instead of staying in the paddock, three of the six bolted over a stone wall and off to freedom; the only taste of it they'd had for two long months. I'd neglected to think about their long trip here. I'd neglected to think about how they had been living on the savannah of drought-ravaged South East Queensland and were now surrounded by lush green pasture, and I'd neglected to realise it was probably colder than they had ever experienced. I chased after the goats and managed to retrieve them. Into a shed they were herded, and there they stayed for two months until new fences were erected and we could safely let them out.

It was a lesson on so many levels, especially about loving gestures. I had thought giving Susan six beautiful cashmere goats was such a charming idea. By the time the goats were purchased, freighted and the new fencing was done, I could have shown my adoration no more expensively by giving her a diamond ring. So, don't just research the animal you are buying – make sure that your set-up is adequate on the fencing and watering levels.

We wanted a supplementary grazing animal that we could run in conjunction with the geese and that would have a use. Cashmere is beautiful, but you need at least 50 kilograms of fleece to even begin processing it, so my visions of du Fermier cashmere wraps were soon put in the too-hard basket.

All animals need daily checks; and, like the poultry, our goats get locked up each night, to make them easy to handle, semi-trained and safe. One of the great things about having them confined for the first two months was that they became very used to us and our daily ministrations. After our experience with the goats, I always keep new livestock close at hand for their first few weeks.

Birthing was also eye opening. Again, it was something that was a very nice idea when 'ordering' the goats, but a little terrifying in reality. Needless to say, we managed. Or, in truth, Hazel and Lady managed for us: Hazel with twins, Lady with a single kid. We are yet to introduce a billy to our ladies, but feel that, when we do, it will be a once-only occurrence. Goats, like geese, live long lives and, as cute as the babies are, they will need tending for many years; and we think that our herd can only sustainably be held at between nine and fifteen.

There are still some days that I weigh up the choice between the diamond or the goats. I know on some days Susan may prefer the thought of the diamond too, but to spend time with these curious, intelligent creatures is a delight. Their sleepy eyes in the morning when you go and wake them up in their stable, as they stretch, stand and gently look for a morning cuddle, melt your heart. Their enthusiastic gallop from wherever they are at dusk when the call of 'Goatie, Goatie, Goaties!' rings out to summon them to bed. And what is the use of having them? Well, for grazing, more bedding for the compost, delightful companionship and fleece.

Cows are a slightly more vexed matter. Why would we want them? It's not as if I can breed them for meat. The first cows we had on the property were a pair of hand-reared Belted Galloways one of my beef suppliers lent to me. Incredibly lovely, but oh so bolshy. I've learned always to be suspicious of a hand-reared farm animal; they have little or no fear of humans and can be very naughty. I've had hand-reared lambs grow up to be as friendly as can be, but when you turn your back, they can drop you in a second, with a well-placed headbutt to the back of the knee. And if the cows decide to take up residence in the goat house because it's wet outside, nothing will change their mind – a belt on the backside with a piece of poly pipe will usually result in a hoof in your thigh.

Cows, even miniature cows, are very big and, no matter how cute they are, need tending. We discovered you have to make sure you are prepared for all the sundry activities around health care and, in the case of Galloways, hair care: they need their ear hair trimmed! Again, when we bought, we chose carefully, favouring the smaller Scottish breeds that enjoy rough terrain and varied diets, which makes them perfect for traversing the gully and helping with blackberry and gorse. And the two that were on loan … had to go home. They traversed the creek one Friday lunchtime and went to visit Mr Bremner, the vegetable farmer. It's not often a farmer strides through the restaurant on a Friday afternoon, bellowing, 'Have Annie's Belties got out?'

So, after much consideration, and erecting some more fencing, we decided on Miniature White Galloways. They have thick, curly white coats and black points, and are on the smaller side. These beasts have a gentle nature, and unlike the hand-reared farm animals, they have just enough nervousness around humans to make them amenable. Still, it took time to get them used to us and able to be handled. Like most of our beasts and birds, bucket training is very important: this means that, in a crisis, a bucket can be rattled and, from all corners of the farm, the animals will come and congregate. In many ways, it is always a peaceful process getting new animals settled on the farm and with us. I have, on occasion, slept in their lodgings or read a book quietly in their presence. Curiosity is part of cows' nature, and, if you sit quietly for long enough, they will come to you, their breath hot on your hands or your neck, depending from which direction they have come. Spending time at night in the house of the goats and cows is both soothing and quietly intoxicating.

Having a bit of land means you can always help out a friend. My friend Paula has a small, and incredibly precious, flock of Gotland sheep. For many years, I have been a great fan of the breed, having the restaurant adorned with their lush, curly grey skins in the winter. My fascination with them is so great that I have even travelled to Gotland and spent time on a small sheep stud, while knowing it is highly unlikely that I would ever be able to keep these animals. It pleases me to know that one of the top rams in Sweden is named Sindarve Jumbuck – a little Australian connection on the other side of the world – and there are several small flocks of Gotland sheep here. Paula's live in New South Wales, and when the combination of drought and the threat of bushfires became too much in the summer of 2020, we were able to accommodate them while her paddocks were resown and improved. This allowed me to almost have some Gotland sheep myself, and also help with preserving and tending a rare breed of animal.

Then there are the ducks, who are a roaming pack of jokers: a couple of mixed breed, a trio of call ducks and a handful of Indian Runners. We keep the ducks for pest control, entertainment and eggs. The composition of a duck egg is quite different from that of a chicken egg, and is splendid when used in the restaurant for cakes and pasta. Runner ducks are prolific layers, but not in nests, like chickens; they tend to just lay anywhere. I look forward to many hours spent in egg hunts as our flock matures.

So, as you can see, the keeping of farm animals is not to be taken lightly, even though on small properties like ours, they are used for grazing and companionship; it's not really like proper farming. A working knowledge of fencing, electric fencing and irrigation is a must. We do take great pride in our beasts and birds and continually lust for more, but are kept in check by commonsense issues such as the need for ever more fencing and ever more troughs that don't have to be filled manually.

I love that we get to be involved in supporting some rare breeds. There is a niche for those who don't want to eat their stock, allowing us to be part of plans supporting breeds that are starting to struggle. I feel that if I can choose to have non-supermarket apple varieties, I can also encourage non-supermarket breeds of lamb and beef.

At times, I find the paradox that I keep no animals for meat but cook meat constantly at the restaurant a little baffling. By combining the two, though, I feel that the knowledge I have gleaned from many of my farmer friends helps me recognise and understand good animal husbandry in both the live animal and the carcass. The re-emergence of small-scale farming, which often specialises in rare breeds, is made viable by the sale of the meat. But this element of biodiversity needs to be continued, so that our farming resources can be used effectively and we can do better by the animals being farmed. Being involved in the preservation of rare breeds helps protect animals that have become less popular, as they, essentially, don't make enough money on the hook. And, as always, the stories behind some of these breeds are as delightful as the animals themselves. Take, for example, the Shropshire sheep. It is famous for being the only sheep that doesn't eat trees and is perfect for grazing in orchards. It is also a solid little unit; excellent for meat, and a favourite with knitters of socks and hats, as the wool is very soft. The breed is in demand in Japan, as its wool is perfect for filling futons.

We also share Babbington with a hoard of domestic animals, as the culmination of melding two households. We have: two brace of British Shorthair cats; two terriers, a Cairn and a Westie; and the new family dog, Moss the labrador. And Taco, the blue budgerigar. As with any blended family, the number of people and animals can sometimes be a bit overwhelming. We had to bring together two completely different views on how domestic animals should exist. Susan's family came with one small dog and a very chatty budgie. The dog is generally well behaved, sleeps in a dog bed on the floor

and does what it is told. My animals are the complete opposite. The two boy cats and the Cairn are all allowed on the bed, and are insubordinate and spoiled. The two girl cats, who are rescues, are fearful, have special needs and sometimes forget their house-training. Three years in, there are compromises, but we manage; they do make a lot of mess, but matter to us in different ways.

As Susan's older daughter negotiates young adulthood, her little dog is part of her; both a talisman from her childhood and a steadying influence. Her younger daughter revels in the company of the labrador, a symbol of the freedom and the space that a country life has brought – the capacity to run, wrestle and throw off the constraints of the city.

My relationship with my crew never changes; I am what is known as an 'animal person'. My love for my familiars is strong and constant. I cannot imagine a life without a four-legged, furry friend. They are my books of secrets, my ever-loving companions, partners in crime. And, while they all have their own distinct personalities, I cannot help flinching at times when I realise that each seems to have absorbed some aspect of my own personality: Kitten with his naughtiness, Tommy with his madness, and Fenn with his quiet strength. In a strange way, they are a mirror in which I can recognise what I put others through, yet get to care for them in a way that I myself would like to be cared for.

I often wonder why I am such a compulsive animal owner. I have a deep love for them all; the turbulent nature of caring for them is part of my, and now our, day-to-day existence. When animals are penned for their own comfort and safety each night, they do not wish to wait to be let out each morning. So, there is always a reason to get up – everybody needs to be released and fed. There is no option of languishing in bed, feeling sorry for oneself, but there is always the possibility of going back to bed when everyone is tended to. Mostly, once that morning communion has taken place, any misery has been vanquished, and the day is there to be enjoyed and tackled. At night, there is sometimes a collision between my restaurant duties and the impending darkness – a fraught time when professional demands and the need to be home to assist with lock-up conflict. But, and perhaps it is the hospitality professional ingrained in me, the moment when all the geese have their bowls of grain at night is one of joy. The honking and squawking is replaced by the contented, rhythmical tapping of their beaks in their feed, not unlike the quiet that descends on a restaurant table in that moment when the food is put down in front of the diners.

Cooking for the critters, and what to do with those roosters

In a perfect world, where I had oodles of time, I would make all of the food that my cats and dogs eat. Alas, it is not the case, but one day it might be.

Dog biscuits for Tommy

1 cup wholemeal flour
1 cup oats
½ cup flax seeds
½–1 cup beef, veal or chicken stock
¼ cup peanut butter

Preheat the oven to 180 °C.

Place the flour, oats and flax seeds in a bowl, and add ½ cup stock and the peanut butter. Mix until you have a strong dough, and add more stock if needed. Roll out on a floured surface to about 1 cm thick. Cut the biscuits into the required shape, place on a parchment-lined tray and bake for 10 minutes. Remove the tray from the oven, turn the biscuits over and cook for another 10 minutes.

Cool on a rack, then store in an airtight container.

Cat biscuits for Kitten

When I buy fish for the restaurant, I always try to buy the fish whole, and I fillet it. For me, this is the way to get the freshest fish. It also gives me a lovely by-product for the animals. I scrape all the bones down to have a good amount of raw fish, and I cook the wings, or collars, so that I can pull all the flesh from them. This is never for me to eat, but is a treat for the cats, the dogs and sometimes the chickens. If I am feeling particularly loving, I might make Kitten some biscuits. This I do with a mix of cooked and raw flesh, but it's also possible to make them from a 300-gram tin of salmon or tuna.

300 g either tinned fish or gleanings from a fish skeleton

1 egg, beaten

2 cups wholemeal flour

Preheat the oven to 180°C.

Place all the ingredients in a stand mixer fitted with a paddle. Mix to form a dough. If it appears too dry, add a little water; if too wet, add a little more flour. It should be a nice consistency to roll.

Roll out to 0.5 cm thick. Cut out biscuits with a small cutter; place on a silicone-lined tray and bake for about 20 minutes. I use a small fish cutter for Kitten's treats.

Chicken aerobics

Our chickens don't all get let out on a daily basis, given that we have several roosters. The chickens left in their pens love to have some stimulation and exercise. We hang food for them just out of reach, so they have to do a little jump to get it. Eventually, they may or may not pull it all down, but they do seem to enjoy the game. We make bundles of all sorts of things from the garden for them. A plant from which we have cut a cauliflower can give five or six chickens a whole day of entertainment, especially if you leave the roots on and the odd grub falls out. At other times of the year, they may get a crisp green and fragrant posy of lettuces, herbs and leaves. Sitting and watching the girls enjoying their greens is one of my favourite things.

For a more sedentary approach to providing the chickens with treats, I am known to sow seed trays with 'chicken mix', available from many seed suppliers. This provides a lovely lush, tasty tray for them to peck at. I am also keen to make them some grazing boxes out of old pallets, a similar treat to the trays of sprouted seeds, but with wire tops so that they can eat the greens but not scratch up the seeds and soil.

What to do with the excess roosters?

It is a sad fact that, in nature, there can only be one boss cock in the chookyard. Come late winter, if not before, the boys will fight, some-times to the death. It is distressing for all and downright dangerous to intervene. If you are hatching out chickens and you have a glut of roosters, you *must* make a plan before it is too late.

As most of them are rare breeds, often they can be sold or given away. Even this can be fraught with danger, though, and we vet any takers carefully, as there is still a problem with cock fighting in Australia.

While we try not to cull anything on the property, sometimes our attempts to get rid of excess roosters fail. Many breeds of fancy egg-laying chickens do not make good meat birds, but some, like the Australorp, are dual purpose. The quicker you can identify if a rooster is destined for the pot, the better. The longer you leave it, the tougher he will become. When he starts crowing is the best time to do the deed. I am a chopper, not a wringer, and use a sturdy block with two 10-centimetre nails banged in 2.5 centimetres apart. I put his little neck between the nails, which helps hold him and guides me; then *bang*, with a sharpened hatchet I have especially for this job. It's not a pleasant task, and it makes me feel sick to the core, but it is done, and done quickly.

The next bit is arduous in a different way. I tie string to the bird's legs and suspend him at chest level, and then set about dry-plucking him. You get better at it with practice. Once I am done, I slip my hand into the cavity, making sure I keep to the outer wall, and collect the innards gently in my hand, and give them a good strong tug to pull them out as a whole. I then wipe the bird clean, inside and out, and swear I will never do that again.

Usually, I will make stock out of my birds if I kill them, which is a cop-out, but …

Once the stock is made, I will shred all the meat off the carcass to give to the animals, so it's not wasted.

Again, farmyard politics are brutal: there can be only one bull, one ram, or one rooster when it's breeding season. Otherwise, the fighting and injuries are horrific. It is a blessing that the boys tolerate the castrati. Except for the geese; they have it all worked out with their marriages – just as long as you don't expect them to share bedrooms.

Weather

I t would be clear by now that challenging weather is not something we are short of at Babbington Park, and is a constant source of fascination and frustration. Our time here has been a very steep learning curve in understanding the nature of weather and the effect that it has on the life that we are invested in.

We have learned the effects of altitude, something that had never even entered my head. There is a basic rule of thumb: for every 100 metres, the temperature drops 1 degree. I feel like I should have known this, with my interest in wine and cheese and the concept of *terroir*, but it never occurred to me when we looked at buying this property. The other small issue that we didn't take into account was that our farm sits at the top of the hill in Lyonville, at about 770 metres above sea level. Being at the highest point in the locale, we tend to collect the worst of the weather, as it spins and spirals up and down the hills. Wind is the weather phenomenon that we see the most, due to our position on the hill. While it bodes well for our sustainable power aspirations in the future, the wind was to be endured, rather than welcomed, in our early years.

On a maintenance level, the wind alerts us to every loose piece of roofing iron and timber on the property. I like to think positively about this, as it leads to a disciplined list of things that need to get done, but at times it is vexing, as we often have to move on to new projects earlier than we hoped, simply so as not to spend money on maintaining something that is falling down – on, essentially, doing a job twice.

The wind is sometimes a battering ram to our souls, as well as our bodies. It is obvious that the madness it sometimes induces in humans, it also induces in animals. They hate it – if they can't find shelter from it, they just turn their backs on the wind and let it wash over them, trying to be at one with it. After high-wind periods, all the animals look a little drained from the effort of coping with it. In the garden, it can be devastating. But while the wind can be destructive, it can also be a teacher, reminding us that all the orchard trees must be tethered to stout stakes by several straps. It is why we have put such thought into the style of hedging that we have placed around both the orchard and the vegetable garden. In time, these hedges will help with filtering the strength of the wind as it reaches our productive garden. The mixed hedgerow that is our first line of defence will merge, as it is a mixture of plants and growing habits. This will encourage an inherent strength that will serve us well in time.

The other thing we have had to come to grips with is that the summer and winter winds are completely different. The cold of the wind in winter can make you feel like the muscle is being stripped from your bones. The summer winds bring fear and trepidation, as at any time they could be bringing the seeds of fire with them if the surrounding hills are alight. They can also bring quick death to new growth in the vegetable garden if plans are not made in advance.

The hostility of the northern winds in summer is part of the reason we have a number of different forms of irrigation in the vegetable garden. On super-windy days, running either the trigger-head or wobble-head sprinklers is a waste of time, as the wind picks up and carries the water away before it has hit the plants or the soil. This is when we switch quickly to dripper lines, so at least we can keep the roots of the plants damp, even if the wind is drying their foliage. Knowing what winds are coming is the key to surviving them, and there is many a morning ritual that has become second nature once we know the forecast. Rolling up the sides of the poly tunnel to allow the wind to travel through; switching the irrigation over to the appropriate delivery system; making sure piles of things that could be dangerous when 'flying' are battened down; and, perhaps most importantly, being tidy. There is nothing more irritating than spending hours trudging around picking up boxes and buckets and stuff that has been blown hither and yon, simply because someone couldn't be bothered putting it away properly.

The cold is the aspect of the weather that we have to give the next most consideration to. I discovered very quickly that our growing season was a great deal shorter than I was used to in Malmsbury. This has meant that we have had to change our expectations of how and when we sow and harvest. The cycle of seeds and plants is tethered to two main internal clocks in the seeds' DNA: the soil and air temperatures, and the day length. It is our soil temperature that is most important here, as our altitude makes it slower to heat up. The first year we were here, we started sowing outside in September, and it was a complete waste of time – everything perished. Now we might start sowing as early as late July or early August, but these plants are often cosseted for months before they are planted outside, after we have spent weeks taking the temperature of the soil, making sure it is safe.

There are aspects of the cold that we can exploit. Plants such as herbaceous peonies, poppies and asparagus all need to have a certain number of days under 7 degrees to really flourish. The sweetness of our parsnips and turnips is enhanced by the depth and the strength of our frosts. The mildness of the climate is also key to why we can grow such good and productive berry crops. While we have snow,  frost and wind, the fact that it doesn't get too hot makes it an ideal climate for berries. On a bleak, windy, freezing Lyonville day, it is always good to have a store of positives to think about. This high above sea level, we can also sit under cloud for days; this is often a still and strange experience, and I am always surprised that I am not quite at ease with it.

Our frosts are heavy and can be damaging, especially in spring, with our fruit trees. I do find that, as the climate is so much cooler than I experienced in Malmsbury, a lot of our bud burst is much slower than it was there and therefore is less likely to be damaged by later frosts, as the plants are so much further behind. We also get snow. In our years here, we have only had one really good dump of snow that settled for days and was many centimetres thick. This is in stark contrast to the stories we hear of snow being around for weeks and Farmer Botheras needing to go to the trouble of laying underground heating pipes so his hothouse could grow food over the winter.

With an average rainfall of above 1100 millimetres, we are in quite a wet part of Victoria. However, the rain doesn't always come when it is needed. The cycles of El Niño and La Niña need to be taken into account each year, so that we can prepare accordingly. Our second summer here was in an El Niño year, which meant that we had no rain at all for a period of fifteen weeks across the late spring and summer. While this was difficult to endure at the time, it has helped us plan infrastructure projects, so that we can handle these difficulties better as they beset us in the future.

We always watch carefully for a La Niña event – an indication that Australia is headed for a wet year, which can be drought break-ing for some and a much-needed boost for the Murray–Darling system. During the horror that was 2020, I certainly hung onto the promise of a La Niña year ahead. Summer 2021 was indeed very cool and reasonably wet; our yields were down and I wore jumpers more often than I would have liked, but thankfully the harrowing parts of the previous summer were missing. La Niña does not automatically lead to less stress, as then there is always a chance of flooding, but for the general health of the environment, it is a welcome sign, often creating flows in parched river systems. I would never have thought ten years ago that I would have a basic working knowledge of the language of climatologists and meteorologists, but have found that it is imperative as we strive to lighten our footprint on the earth.

The heat in summer is my least favourite weather to manage. Perhaps it is because I am not a natural heat seeker, preferring milder and cooler weather. Over the years, I have adjusted to the temperature of kitchens in the warmer months – often arriving at work early in the morning and leaving in the late afternoon/early evening, which means I seem not to notice the heat escalating during the day – but I don't find gardening in the summer much fun. To circumnavigate it, I use the outlying hours to complete my outdoor tasks. There are approximately five more hours of daylight in January than there are in June and I put the peripheral hours to good use. As weeding, watering and harvesting are our main jobs in the summer, I generally rise early, and water and pick vegetables after I have tended to the animals' needs. The hours in the late afternoon can be pleasantly spent, moving up and down the rows hand-weeding and hand-watering, with a broad-brimmed hat and something interest-ing to listen to; it's a productive and calming way to spend the last hours of the day.

We are lucky here in Central Victoria to see very distinct seasons. They are driven by the weather patterns at hand, and while they differ a little from one year to the next, they are still identifiable. As we have a large area of land to grow our food on, we can revel in the seasonality of food, and relish those fruits and plants that are only perfect for a few weeks at a time. There is the snap of an asparagus spear in the cool of an October morning; the sweetness of a strawberry, slightly warm from its day in the sun, on a late-March afternoon; the sense of achievement as your cold fingertips break brussels sprouts off the stem on a June afternoon, as the wind and the rain whip around you; the bucolic sense of achievement as you take in the productivity of the vegetable patch at dusk in January. Again, I often refer to the Gariwerd weather periods, as they describe what we experience here much better than the European seasons.

The sensory experiences attached to all weather conditions make you realise how alive you are – how much there is to find joy in. Weather is not something that simply dictates what you wear on any given day; for me, it is a maelstrom that gives meaning and importance to so much of what I do.

Recipes to warm up, cool down and stay hydrated

There are a number of go-to recipes I have that dissipate the effects of the weather on my body and my mind. If I need to quickly seek respite from wind, rain or heat, I will always just duck inside and have a cup of tea. I am a voracious tea drinker and, when all else fails, it tends to be my fixer: a pot of Yorkshire Gold loose-leaf tea, brewed in an iconic Robur silver teapot under a blue-and-white cosy knitted by my mother, always does the trick.

Tea aside, I have a real interest in the science of eating appropriately for different weather conditions. Of course, there are many lovely and

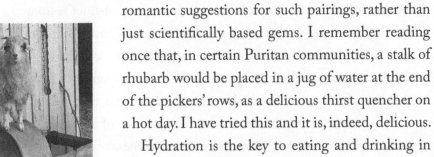

romantic suggestions for such pairings, rather than just scientifically based gems. I remember reading once that, in certain Puritan communities, a stalk of rhubarb would be placed in a jug of water at the end of the pickers' rows, as a delicious thirst quencher on a hot day. I have tried this and it is, indeed, delicious.

Hydration is the key to eating and drinking in hot weather. It is always good to stay away from foods that take a great deal of energy to digest. Those that are high in protein, fibre and sugar are hard work for the body and are best avoided. I find when I am out in the garden, as well as having ample water on hand, I like to snack on the things around me: I'll munch on a cucumber, pluck some iceberg lettuce or gather a handful of strawberries. All these foods are high in water and easy to digest.

In cold weather, the opposite applies. Look for food that demands energy to digest. This is a process known as thermogenesis, where the heat is produced in the body by metabolising food. There is nothing more sustaining and warming than a good bowl of porridge on a winter's morning before a day outside in the cold. Equally warming is a bowl of beef and pumpkin stew when you come inside. A super-quick way of warming up is to drink ginger tea, as it heats you from within and is also excellent for stimulating thermogenesis.

The wind affects people differently. It makes me a little anxious and very crochety. There is no real scientific evidence to explain this effect on people, but there is much speculation about it. Because the wind makes me feel this way, I tend to eat foods that are known to help with relieving anxiety, which are also often anti-inflammatory foods.

One of the things that we do know about wind – which is particularly clear when we observe plants and our own skin – is that it is extremely dehydrating. The hot weather and cold weather can both cause issues with hydration, in different ways. If your personal hydration is on point, this allows your system, both physical and mental, to cope with the vagaries of the weather.

Porridge

This is a very basic porridge recipe that allows you to add your own embellishments. It is made in the traditional Scottish manner with water, not milk, allowing you to add a little cream on serving. It is made with medium oatmeal, not rolled oats, giving an authentic texture. Salt is always needed in porridge, as it brings out the wonderful natural flavour of the oatmeal. If you have plenty of stores from your summer garden, this is the time to get them out: honey from your bees; berries, either in the form of a conserve, or a compote that has been frozen. Roasted nuts, or even candied nuts, add texture. Imagine almonds candied in honey with bottled peach slices bringing a summery golden light to a cold grey morning in the middle of winter. Porridge needs to be eaten as soon as it is ready and should always be stirred with a proper spurtle.

Put 3 cups of water in a small saucepan. Add 1 cup of medium oatmeal and cook on a medium heat, bring to the boil and stir constantly. When you see the porridge start to move, add ½ tsp of salt flakes. Keep cooking, stirring all the while, for another couple of minutes. It needs to cook for about 5 minutes from when you add the salt. Pour into a bowl, and serve with cream or milk, and anything else that takes your fancy.

If you don't eat it all, the porridge can be spread on a tray and cut into cakes. These can then be fried in butter, and served with butter and jam, honey or golden/maple syrup later on.

Iranian noodle soup

This soup has become a staple in our house. Living in a more rural setting, where the closest shops are a fair way away, we always have a good stockpile of tinned beans and pulses. This soup, which is often served during the Persian new year in late March, is quick, easy and surprisingly delicious. I mean surprising in that its ingredient list is very simple, so the complexity of the soup is unexpected. It is also incredibly nourishing in hot or cold weather, and the use of turmeric and addition of yoghurt give it anti-anxiety and anti-inflammatory properties.

2 onions
50 ml olive oil
2 tsp ground turmeric
3 garlic cloves, finely chopped
400-g tin chickpeas, drained
400-g tin small brown lentils, drained
400-g tin haricot beans, drained
1 L vegetable stock
100 g linguine
200 g spinach
30 g fresh parsley
20 g fresh coriander
20 g fresh mint
100 ml plain yoghurt

Dice the onions. Heat the olive oil in a large pan over a medium heat, and fry the diced onions for 5 minutes, or until soft, and pale golden in colour. Add the turmeric and garlic and cook for a further 4 minutes.

Add the chickpeas, lentils and haricot beans to the onions and pour in the stock. Simmer for 30 minutes, stirring occasionally.

When the beans have simmered for 30 minutes, add the linguine to the pot and cook for a further 10 minutes.

Roughly chop the spinach on a board, along with the parsley, coriander and mint.

Stir the spinach and herbs into the noodles and beans. Serve with a streak of yoghurt on top. If you're vegan, omit the yoghurt and add a squeeze of lemon and a drizzle of olive oil.

Tomato kasoundi

I try to make large batches of this in the last days of summer and into the autumn. The kasoundi is a perfect reminder of the heat of summer, especially when eaten in the cold of winter.

60 g green chillies, chopped with or without seeds
125 g garlic, peeled and chopped
250 g fresh ginger, peeled and chopped
500 ml malt vinegar
250 ml grapeseed oil
90 g black mustard seeds
30 g turmeric powder
90 g cumin powder
60 g chilli powder
2 kg ripe tomatoes
75 g salt
250 g brown sugar

Mince the chillies, garlic and ginger in a food processor with 50 ml vinegar. Set aside.

Heat oil in a large heavy-bottomed pot until very hot. Add spices and stir for about 5 minutes.

Add garlic mix. Cook for another 5 minutes, stirring constantly.

Add tomatoes, salt, vinegar and sugar and cook for 60–90 minutes, until the oil has come to the top and the kasoundi is thick.

Bottle in sterilised jars.

Summer salads

The food I eat through the summer is mainly based on salads for which I can collect the ingredients from the garden, augmented with lean protein like chicken, and spices, nuts, apple cider vinegar and yoghurt. There are no real recipes for these salads, and, given the scope of what we grow, there are many variations.

Some of my favourite combinations are: chicken, chermoula, cucumber, lettuce and roasted almonds, with apple cider vinegar and yoghurt; lightly blanched French beans, fresh tomato, Ligurian olives, salad leaves, a little olive oil and lemon juice; Lyonnaise salad with poached egg, bread croutes, bacon, Frisée lettuce and sherry vinaigrette; hot smoked trout, pickled red onions, salad leaves, radish, pickled turnip and yoghurt.

Other times in the summer, I might make myself only a little platter of raw vegetables, hummus, bread and salumi. My eating habits are quite different in the summer. In winter, I am often starving by six o'clock and desperate to sit down to dinner, but in summer, breakfast and lunch are the two main meals for me. I will often come home from work, have a cup of tea and then head out into the garden until dusk. By that stage, I have no real interest in dinner and will frequently just come in and head off to bed.

The decorative
garden

OF ALL THE many delightful things at Babbington Park, it is the decorative garden that gives me the most joy. But, as a purely ornamental pocket of the property, it can be a very long way down the list of priorities. Sometimes this vexes me, but it is a reality that must be borne. It is a constant surprise that it fills me with such pleasure, especially as it's an area I feel poorly skilled in.

When Susan and I moved here, we struggled with digesting and processing the scale of the place. The size of everything that we do now is bigger than either of us was used to: more buildings to work on, more hectares to tend; more water needed, more infrastructure to install.

I had gardened almost half a hectare at Malmsbury and, years before, a lovely plot of a similar size on a steep hill in Daylesford. Susan had tended gardens that were of a comparable size. A house and driveway area that spanned a good part of what the eye could see was something new to the both of us, and we both knew it was important that we didn't get the garden wrong.

Very early in the piece, we were lucky enough to have my dear friend Paul, the extraordinary landscape designer, gift us a rough plan for this garden. He understands the concept of scale; when he first saw the property, he was entranced by the view of the water and the fall of the land. In discussing what we wanted, I raised several ideas that I had in mind. They included a flat lawn in front of the house that ended with a ha-ha wall (a sort of infinity pool suitable for lawns, and a way to have animals grazing in the paddock below without the need for fences, or them escaping into the garden); and massive perennial and annual borders. I remember ribbing him about not having any of those fussy box balls and all that – I wanted him to get his Vita Sackville-West on. This has given us a plan to work from, but, as yet, the final structure of the garden is far from decided. The plan also includes a couple of buildings that we have since abandoned the notion of constructing, which means reimagining the borders and access points. Most importantly, it gives us a blueprint that has measurements on it, so I can keep doodling to scale, rubbing out and starting again. I would highly recommend that when planning a decorative garden on a large scale, you at least have a chat to a professional, as it can be so helpful as you move forwards. A good landscape designer knows how the land sits within itself, how beauty can be superimposed on the natural attributes of the ground, and can give you an idea of scale and proportion.

One of the pluses for us is that the house is positioned a long way back from the road and in the centre of the north/south indices. There is one little anomaly in that there is a second residence that was once attached to the property. Some years ago, this house and the hectare or so of land around it was split off and sold. It means that we share part of a driveway, and there is a sort of C-shaped chunk out of the front of the farm.

The land that leads from the road to the house is relatively flat, before it falls away down the hill to the lake. Given that we shared part of a driveway with our neighbour, and it went past the potato shed and the green sheds, we decided in our first year that we would create a new entrance. This was done on the south side. A drive was graded, and our waste concrete was crushed and added to the road base, with crushed rock for the topping. A hedgerow of Washington Thorns was planted at the front, in a nod to the hawthorns that proliferate as hedging in the area, and a gateway was installed.

Susan collects old Sunshine gates. These gates were manufactured by HV McKay, the early Australian industrialist who developed the Sunshine Harvester, whose metalworks went on to produce and

distribute gates. They evoke nostalgia, as many
of them date from the early 20th century. One of
Susan's beloved Sunshine gates has been used for
the entrance, and there are wings made out of my
favourite French chestnut and wire fencing. Down
the driveway, we have planted an avenue of Algerian
oaks, which are quick growing and a delightful
specimen tree. We chose these because they will form

a lovely canopy and avenue in the decades to come. Our neighbour to
the south built quite close to the boundary, so we have planted a line
of evergreen hedging to create a little privacy. We have retained the
existing driveway, and found that this area doubles as outside storage
for rocks, posts, wire, poly pipe, fencing materials, portable animal
houses and the like. It fulfils the role of the trade entrance, so that we
can store the farm's needs in an accessible and tidy way.

As you arrive at the end of both driveways, you come into a
rectangular forecourt area. From here, you can access the church,
the shearing shed, the house, the brick shed and the garage. It is the
nexus of the property. A local stonemason has transformed a fairly
rough-and-ready circle at the centre of the area. As at various points
on the periphery of the forecourt there is a series of old stone walls,
we have continued this theme and had a low stone-walled circle constructed around that central bed. Not only is it a nod to the historical
walls, but it uses up the same resource that our forebears were using
up: the enormous amount of stone that we keep turning over. When
it was decided that Mum was coming to live in the church, we
commissioned a rectangular stone wall and garden bed in front of it.

When it comes to the rest of the pretty garden, there has not been
much progress. It is slow going, as we are always waiting for men with
machines to turn up. We need an excavator here or a Bobcat there, and
it is like a game of chess trying to line up the pieces so we can move

forwards. The six very large cypresses that were at the northern end were cut down one October. They were removed because they were very large, very scrappy and hindered the view of our magnificent manna gum. As they were on the northern side, they also blocked out a great deal of sun from the back garden, and we are enjoying the different light we now have at the back of the house. It wasn't until the following May that the man arrived to remove the stumps, and the Bobcat man has been by to do a little levelling and neatening.

I have realised that getting cross about, or frustrated by, these delays is a poor use of my energy. What I do while I am waiting for these works to be done is learn. I have been teaching myself how to construct a planting plan and how to propagate decorative plants from seed. Learning these things not only helps save my sanity but is kind to my wallet. I soon realised when I started mapping out plans and beds that the garden was going to require thousands of plants. Just to buy perennials, bulbs and annuals for the round garden in the forecourt cost well over $500. The cost of planting out the whole garden at this level would be many, many times this. It has been in my vested interest to research the plants I like, acquire seed and start them off in the poly tunnel, and then find holding rows for them in the vegetable patch until I need to use the plants.

The waiting game has other pluses. Not only am I sitting on nursery stock of hundreds of plants, but it allows us the time to actually live in and experience the space. Where do we like to sit in the summer? Where does the light filter in during the winter? Do we need access at this point or that? It has also given us the space to form a relationship with the area that we live in. If I had had the cash, I might have immediately had the whole site levelled as soon as we were gifted the garden plan. I am glad that this was not the case. While there are some patches that definitely need straightening out, I am at peace with the sway of the land and wish to work with its topography, as opposed to re-forming it. The delays have also alerted us to where and how vehicles need to move around the property, whether it be the hay-cutting equipment or something as banal as the route we push the wheelbarrow along to get wood to the house.

I doubt that it will ever be a grandly designed garden, but hopefully it will reflect the personalities of those who live here, with a little touch of Paul. My planting palette is, unashamedly, partial to the English cottage garden. Having grown up with a native-focused garden, I cannot quite find the love for that style. I love wild and abundant climbing roses; fluffy poppies, full of ruffles and frills; delphiniums, foxgloves and salvias; the silvery greys of Nepeta, Echinops and Eryngium. The climate here can support the romantic abundance of an English cottage garden, which suits my somewhat chaotic aesthetic. For all the structure and discipline that I apply to the planting and formation of the vegetable garden, it is gentle disarray that I am looking for in our house garden.

Another stipulation when creating our own garden space is that it needs to be as low maintenance as possible. Once we have added our domestic garden to the overall plan, we will have over 2 hectares under gardening, mowing, hedging and pruning regimens – more than enough for two women in their fifties, I say. This means that a fair portion of it will be given over to grassed areas that are easy to mow, with garden beds that are full of self-seeding plants, as well as perennials that only need trimming once a year. In my mind, I can see it through the seasons: the soft pinks, greens, blues and silvers that start to emerge in spring; to the golden, browned and slightly decayed look of the seed heads and spent plants in the winter. This allows the decorative plants a life span that their productive cousins could only dream of.

And, as much as I love the idea of having a posh garden, I am not sure whether I can afford it, or, when I really question myself, if it would reflect who we are. However, I am forever grateful for Paul's advice, gentle guidance, and exasperated acceptance of my inability to prioritise paths and prettiness over vegetables. There are many financial hurdles to leap over in trying to live a more sustainable life. I am finding one of the keys to navigating this curious steeplechase is to recognise your personal priorities. For me, it is the vegetables, fruit and building works. Then will come alternative power sources. In the meantime, I keep chipping away at the flowers, growing more nursery stock, constantly running scenarios of wisteria walks by Susan.

The decorative garden brings me joy because its real purpose is to bring beauty into our lives. That is a wonderful thing. It is my hobby, my leisure activity. The vegetable garden takes a lot of my time and is always connected to work and to being disciplined. The soft, luxurious textures of the flowers I fancy simply make me smile to my core.

Recipes for pretty things

There have been many times in my life when I have cooked with flowers and decorative herbs. My earliest memory of this is from the 1970s. My mother would have big parties in summer, and one of my jobs was to ball the halved watermelon and go into the garden to collect borage flowers to decorate the fruit. Their wonderful contrast of vibrant pink and bright blue is seared into my memory as a sign of long, carefree summers. And the taste of the borage flower's sweet nectar probably gave me my first inkling of why bees are attracted to flowers. As I matured, there was the rose geranium–flavoured junket at Stephanie's Restaurant; the use of violas, calendulas and other pretty flowers as garnishes at Lake House; and then the zenith of my cooking with flowers, at Lavandula, a beautiful lavender farm in Central Victoria. From lavender-flavoured scones, to sausages, to cordials, I prepared it all.

The flowers are an extremely important part of our operations. The more flowers that we have in the garden, the more bees we attract and the better the pollination rates we have throughout. While I love them all for their beauty and joyfulness, there are also many that I will happily take into the kitchen and use in my cooking.

Scented bavarois

I have to confess that I have never been a big fan of the panna cotta, a set dairy dessert favoured by the Italians. I lean much more to the slightly more complex bavarois beloved of the French. However, whatever your preferences, they are both wonderful candidates for a scented treatment. This takes place while you are heating the dairy component, and the milk or cream can be infused with all manner of things: lavender and honey, rose petals and vanilla, lemon myrtle, lemon verbena, rose-scented geranium leaves – even violets.

Here is a basic bavarois recipe for you to flavour at will. The stronger flowers and herbs will infuse flavour in half an hour or so; the more gentle ones may take a few hours.

SERVES 6
375 ml milk
4 egg yolks
110 g sugar
4 leaves gelatine
500 ml cream

Bring the milk to scalding point with your chosen scented herbs or flowers (or leave plain). Allow to infuse for at least ½ hour.

Beat the yolks and sugar together until pale yellow. Soak the gelatine in cold water till soft.

Pour the milk onto the egg mix, and return to a clean saucepan and cook, stirring constantly, until thickened. Remove from the heat and add the – well-squeezed-out – gelatine leaves.

Strain into a large, clean mixing bowl and let cool, stirring occasionally to cool it evenly. (This process can be speeded up by cooling it over a bowl of iced water.) When cool, whip the cream to soft peaks and fold into the custard mix. Pour into appropriate moulds and refrigerate overnight.

Floral lavash

225 g plain flour
1 tsp salt flakes and a little extra for baking
1 tsp caster sugar
1 tsp nigella seeds, or poppy or sesame
60 ml olive oil and a little extra for baking
125 ml water
handful rose petals and violas

Preheat oven to 170°C.

Place all dry ingredients in a mixing bowl.

Combine the oil and water, and add to the dry ingredients. Mix together until it forms a soft dough.

Wrap and rest the dough for ½ hour before rolling.

Line 4 baking sheets with baking paper. Divide the dough into 8 rectangles; roll each one out as thinly as possible. Scatter with petals and place another piece on top. Transfer the rolled dough onto the baking paper on the trays and roll again until it is almost translucent and the petals stretched. Then give the biscuits a very light drizzle of olive oil and a little sprinkle of salt.

Bake for 15–20 minutes until golden brown; check halfway through in case you need to turn the trays.

Cool on a wire rack, and store in an airtight container for up to 4 weeks.

Floral summer butter

This is a bit of a party trick, but it always makes people smile. While it uses butter, if you prefer a dip-type dish, you could use cream cheese that has been mixed with a little slow-roasted garlic. Either way, it is a kaleidoscope of colour and flavours.

½ cup room-temperature, best-quality unsalted butter, whipped a little until fluffy
small or torn fresh herb leaves: thyme, dill, flat-leaf parsley, tarragon, sage, chive tips
petals from edible flowers: anise hyssop, marigolds, pansies, calendulas, nasturtiums, Johnny-jump-ups, chive flowers, borage
flaked sea salt
pepper
cracked, roasted coriander seeds, red chilli flakes and poppy seeds

On a platter or board, smear the butter 3 mm thick, using an offset spatula. Scatter generously with the herb leaves, flower petals, salt and pepper. Add cracked coriander seeds, chilli flakes and poppy seeds. Serve with baguette slices.

Crystallised petals

Crystallised rose petals and violets are another vestige of my youth. In my childhood, they were one of the most romantic things I could possibly imagine. They are fiddly, but not difficult, to make. You just need a really good dose of patience.

1 egg white
1 tsp water
caster sugar
rose petals or violets

Lay a piece of baking paper on a tray. In a bowl, whisk the egg white with water until it's a little frothy. Dip the flowers into the egg white mix and lift out, allowing as much excess to drain off as possible. Then use a small spoon to scatter the sugar over each side of the flowers. Place on the baking paper and dry for 24 hours. Store in an airtight container.

Rose water and orange blossom water

These two liquids are commercially available products that stem directly from the decorative garden. Both are represented in Middle Eastern, North African and European cuisines. When using rose or orange blossom water in the myriad recipes that feature them, it is always a lovely touch to garnish the dish with fresh versions of the flowers. Roses are a little easier to find than orange blossoms, but if you have an orange tree, you will already know the bewitching scent that comes from the flowers.

I often include orange blossom water in a sugar syrup that I use on an orange syrup cake, or in this baklava.

Pistachio and orange blossom baklava

MAKES 25 PORTIONS
200 ml water
90 g honey infused with orange blossom
250 g sugar

2 tbsp orange blossom water
1 packet filo sheets
100 g melted butter
250 g ground pistachios

Make the syrup by placing the water, honey, sugar and orange blossom water in a saucepan, and bringing to the boil for 5 minutes, stirring to dissolve the sugar, then simmering for 5 minutes. Remove from the heat and allow to cool.

Preheat the oven to 180°C. I use a 24 × 24 cm cake tin, so you need a tin that has an approximate area of 570 square cm. Cut the filo sheets to the size of the tin. Brush the sides and bottom of the tin with melted butter. You need a minimum of 22 sheets (up to 36) depending on the height of the tin. I do 8–5–5–5–8.

Take 1 filo sheet cut to tin size, brush with melted butter, place on the bottom of the tin; repeat, to have 8 layers of pastry. Add a layer of ground pistachios. Take a filo sheet, brush with melted butter, lay on top of the ground pistachios buttered side down, and butter the top side. Add 4 more layers, for 5 layers in total.

Add a layer of ground pistachios. Take a filo sheet, brush with melted butter, lay on top of the ground pistachios buttered side down, and butter the top side. Add 4 more layers, for 5 layers in total. Add a layer of ground pistachios. Take a filo sheet, brush with melted butter, lay on top of the ground pistachios buttered side down, and butter the top side.

Add another 7 buttered sheets, so you have 8 layers in total.

Cut the diamond pattern with a sharp knife.

Bake for 40 minutes. When golden, remove from the oven and immediately pour the syrup over it. Let stand for 8 hours before serving.

Quail with couscous and rose petals

I love the combination of small birds and roses. This dish has Moroccan roots. As a vegetarian option, the quail can be replaced with thickly sliced eggplants marinated in the spice mix and grilled or fried.

12 quail (this is based on 1½ quail per person; if you're hungry,
    go for 2 quail each)
1 tbsp rose water
3 tsp ground cumin
3 tsp ground cinnamon
60 ml fresh lemon juice
2 tbsp olive oil
flaked salt and freshly ground black pepper
3 tbsp crabapple jelly
1 tsp white wine vinegar
1 garlic clove, crushed
1 tbsp finely chopped mint
petals from 2 unsprayed pink or red roses

For the cucumber salad
½ red onion, thinly sliced
4 short (Lebanese) cucumbers
2 tsp fresh lemon juice
1 tbsp olive oil
1 bird's eye chilli, chopped

For the couscous
500 ml water
500 g couscous
60 g unsalted butter
75 g currants
75 g toasted pine nuts

Remove the backbones from your quail. This is best done by inserting a cook's knife into the cavity of the quail and crunching down on either side of the backbone. Turn the quail over, and flatten by pressing forcefully with the palm of your hand.

Combine the rose water, cumin, cinnamon, lemon juice, 1 tbsp oil, salt and pepper in a large bowl, then add the quail and toss to coat. Marinate for a couple of hours. The quail can be cooked in a frying pan, on a ribbed grill or on a barbecue – it's up to you, just make sure the pan or grill plate is hot. Cook the butterflied quail, skin side down, for 2–3 minutes or until golden, then turn and cook for a further 4–6 minutes until cooked through. (If you have limited space, you can seal off the quail in batches on the stovetop, then finish them on a baking tray in a preheated 180 °C oven for 5 minutes.)

To make the cucumber salad, place the onion, cucumber, lemon juice, oil and chilli in a bowl and gently toss to combine.

To make the couscous, bring the water to the boil and add a good pinch of salt. Mix in the couscous, then work the butter through it gently with a fork. Add the currants and pine nuts, and season to taste with salt and pepper. Set aside for 10 minutes, then fluff it up with a fork.

Stir together the jelly, vinegar, garlic and remaining oil in a small saucepan over a low heat for 1–2 minutes to form a fragrant glaze. Stir in the mint.

Spoon the couscous onto a large serving platter and arrange the quail on top. Pour the glaze over, scatter with rose petals and serve the cucumber salad on the side.

Arts, crafts and sensibilities

PERHAPS IT IS the contentment I have found in my new life at Babbington that has led me to take up pursuits that sometimes surprise even me. They are activities that are linked with trying to waste as little as we can, be it resources or building material, in clothing choices or leisure activities, with a leaning towards – what I almost shudder to call – wholesome solutions.

I have long admired the Shaker communities of North America. Their commitment to craftsmanship is breathtaking; their refusal of modern technology is starting to make a little more sense to me; but it is their ability to work with the natural world and with each other, without greed, that most of my admiration stems from. I often look to their practices for inspiration.

Out in the yard, we pursue all manner of sustainable practices in our pursuit of treading more gently on the earth. Take trellising in the vegetable garden. We are lucky enough to have neighbours with a huge hazelnut hedge. Our own hazelnuts will take a few years to get to the size where we can cut switches from them, but our neighbours' trees are over twenty years old. Each spring, their hedge man comes to trim them, which means, each year, we ask politely if we can have the switches. Hazelnut is beautifully lissom, and we use it to make hoops and arches, stands and teepees for our climbing beans in the summer. It all gets shaped and tied with string; at the end of the season, we pull it all out, store it and keep it for the next year, just in case we don't get enough fresh stuff.

For some of our feature paddock fences, we re-use wood that many would throw away. Where we want a decorative flourish at gateways, we use a combination of old farm hardwood fence 'droppers' and sawn-off recycled palings from pulled-down fences. These are attached to a new framework but provide us with a decorative finish, while using up and showcasing materials that would otherwise have been put on someone's burn pile. They have the added advantage of being replaceable if a cow backs into the gateway and breaks one. As long as the framework is sound, the use of older timbers is a great option, and can add a great deal of character without much expense.

Recycling of products is at the forefront of our mulching practices. The restaurant produces a fair amount of cardboard waste, be it wine boxes or packaging that meat and dairy is delivered in. The cardboard is brought home, denuded of its plastic and sticky tape and stored in the shed. When we clean up the paths in our vegetable gardens, we always lay down cardboard first and then put mulch on top. The cardboard starves the weeds of light and encourages them to die. This practice is repeated on perennial crops, such as the artichokes and the asparagus, to minimise our weeding. When laying the new hedges in the house garden or planting trees, we always interlock cardboard around the plants and then cover it with mulch. At peak times, we don't have enough cardboard, so this means a trip to our local pharmacist, who regularly offers his cardboard to the local community.

The mulch that we use on top of our cardboard comes from various sources connected to the farm. As I mentioned earlier, there were two stands of enormous, and quite straggly, cypresses here when we bought Babbington. After we'd been here a couple of years, the six trees in the backyard were the first to go, as they blocked out a great deal of light and, more importantly, were encroaching on the majestic old manna gum. They were not trees that could be clear-felled, or removed by an excavator, given their position – which, in hindsight, I am hugely grateful for. The trees were cut down by an arborist with a hand-held chainsaw and then put through a chipper. Truckload after truckload of cypress chip mulch was deposited in a holding bay, to season and be used at a later date. I thought it would take us forever to use it all, but within eight months, there was none left and I am greedily eyeing the other stand of cypresses, wondering when they can be dispatched as well. If we'd been able to clear-fell them, I would have missed out on all that mulch.

Straw is another product we use for mulching. For some crops, we choose to buy good-quality pea straw that has a once-only application. We also buy small rounds of barley or oaten straw for the bedding of the geese, goats and cattle, and the outsides of these rolls often get wet and are not suitable for bedding, and are perfect for use as a general garden mulch. They may throw a little seed, and it is a little more difficult for the seeds to germinate if placed on cardboard. For those that defy the odds, given the geese's and ducks' voracious appetite for grass, such weeds don't last long at our place.

Metal bending is one of my new pursuits at Babbington. Our garden uses an enormous number of stakes and pegs. With all the nets and covers, and peonies and delphiniums that need a little support in the wind, we have moved away from buying mass-produced pegs and supports, and make them ourselves. It is fairly easy to find a bench-top wire bender. Having this natty little device that cost me a little over $100, plus a roll of 4-millimetre-thick wire and some bolt cutters, means that we can make pegs and supports to any size and specifications that we need. It beats running to the hardware store to buy them but also creates a product that is easier to use than a hand-bent piece of wire. We find that, particularly with our big fruit nets, a wide peg with two proper right angles hammers into the ground with a great deal more efficiency and efficacy than does a more haphazardly shaped one.

My love affair with metal doesn't end there. While perusing the internet one night, I came across a company in England that had won a prize at the Chelsea Flower Show for its plant hoops and supports. I tried to replicate them on my little bender, but to no avail. So I asked a clever friend of mine to make me a 'jig' – the pattern for shaping metal around. We bought 6-millimetre steel rods that are clamped and rolled around the jig to form wonderful garden hoops. There is enough inherent strength in these hoops to run twelve down a pair of beds, with seven to eight runs to a block. These hoops support our insect netting, to keep our crops of brassicas a little safer from cabbage moths, and our strawberries safe from birds and the naughty labrador who becomes a strawberry thief in summer. With both the wire bending and the steel rod bending, we are using products that we will get at least ten years' use out of, making them a far better alternative than many options on the market.

Rocks are another resource that we hoard. As on most properties, we are always finding more when we turn over soil. The rocks are collected, and sorted into piles based on size. Then we always have this resource on hand when needed for various projects. For example, when the 'deck' around the goose pond was made, the area was back-filled, covered in cardboard and chip mulch, and we are slowly filling it with found rocks of up to fist size. This is because the water fowl have a tendency to pick up everything around the pond and put it in the water. If we use stones that are too big for them to pick up but not too big to walk on, we get a decorative finish, a use for some of our stones, and don't have a pond full of mud and stones. The rest of the piles will be used for stone walling, paths and even some of the restorative works on the spring, where we can add stones to the water's path to help prevent the silt from building up.

There is no denying that I have quite a busy life. Between the restaurant and the property and my various extracurricular activities,

I have made a choice about how much downtime I am happy with. Managing your time is one of the cornerstones of sustainable living; if the work–life balance is out of whack, parts of your life will become unsustainable. One of the key aspects of preventing this is choice. I choose to run my life in the way that I do and accept the consequences when they come. I know that if I put myself under too much financial pressure, my mental health suffers. I know if I create too many deadlines in one clump, that's another trigger for mental health issues. Doing too much, eating poorly, sleeping poorly can all affect the efficacy with which I work and relate to others. Given that the bulk of my work is performance-based, I need to keep on top of these things, or I will start a downward cycle that can be hard to reverse.

When hobbies become jobs – like my gardening, or perhaps even my animal keeping – where do I go for leisure activities? The simplest answer to this is that, for me, leisure activities have become activities with purpose. This creates a mind shift that allows us to see the gardening and animal keeping as joyous activities that are part of our leisure and not more work.

This attitude also influences our indoor pursuits. When we discovered that it would take years to accumulate enough cashmere to take to the mill to be processed, I started needle-felting balls. This is the process of repeatedly stabbing wool with a barbed needle and building up layers into spheres. Maybe doing this sounds ridiculous, but crafting beautiful cashmere balls seems to do it for me. They are wondrously textural, being soft and strangely comforting. Also, the process is fraught with danger, making it quietly aggressive and very rewarding. I am often found at night-time, in the chair by the fire, rhythmically stabbing bundles of cashmere. Various Facebook tableaus inspired my brief flirtation with harvesting hair from all the British Shorthair cats and felting it into balls, until my family decreed it was too disgusting. I have to agree that there is something NQR about this, but it does illustrate that even the hair that animals shed can have a purpose. When the world wasn't full of disposable-fashion factories, I am sure many a community would hoard and gather all manner of fur and hair, and felt it, either with water or barbed objects, to create thick pads of fabric for a variety of uses: clothing, heat-resistant utensil holders, sanitary products, saddle blankets, bags, etc.

Monocropping and intensive farming have had devastating effects on rare-breed flocks and herds across the world. The yarn and fibre industries are at a similar crossroads as the food industry, in terms of making choices about sustainable futures. Clothing, or, rather, the repair of clothing, has become another activity with purpose for us. Susan has taken up darning, and both of us tend to buy clothes of a quality that will ensure they last a long time. Given that my legs are not terribly long, and my pants often need to be taken up, I keep the offcuts for patches in case they are needed later on. I have an awful tendency to wear even my 'good' clothes outside to do jobs, and always seem to get things caught on a nail or a fence and make holes in them. Susan then diligently darns them. I wear my darned clothes with pride, taking inspiration from *sashiko*, the traditional Japanese art of fabric repair. When you get dressed in the morning, there is no more empowering and positive way to start the day than to know where and how your clothes were made.

And we are making the same changes to our day-to-day existence as many others are. We are constantly aware of our use of plastic, so we utilise bamboo toothbrushes, re-usable containers for storing food, products that come in glass, toothpastes and face cleansers that don't contain microplastics ... on and on the list goes.

While I don't eat meat at home, there are beneficial practices I follow with it at work. It is not imperative to keep everything swaddled in cling wrap. Fresh items such as chicken, duck and fish are best left uncovered in the refrigerator. With all three, the drying of their skin makes for a much crisper and crunchier result when cooked. It is not uncommon for restaurant chefs to dry-age duck and beef in their coolrooms for weeks, to improve the product. As a chef, I am very aware of the importance of keeping food at the right temperature. If a domestic fridge is neatly ordered and with good air circulation, it will hold its temperature better and therefore food will keep for longer – ergo, less wastage.

Landfill is a contentious issue, so we are very conscious of our waste levels. This is heightened by the fact that rubbish and recycling collection is only once a fortnight in the country. All food scraps are composted, packaging is kept to a minimum by us growing a lot of our food, and animal food and staple dry goods are bought in bulk. Our cooking utensils must be built to last; we avoid cheap pans and saucepans that are semi-disposable, and are learning to adapt recipes to our bakeware by using simple maths to work out the required areas.

There are certainly some peculiarities in our approach to some basic household items. Living in a very cold, wet area, we cannot dry by hand all the washing the restaurant creates, so we invested in a heat pump dryer. Having never owned a dryer before, this was a big decision for me. The water collected from the clothes is tipped back into the well, and I then do something quite peculiar with the lint collected from them. The house is heated by wood fires, so we used to purchase firelighters to assist with the starting process. Susan likes the convenience of the firelighter, but I have never been a big fan of them. In the age of online media, inked newspaper – the fire starter of my youth – is no longer an option, so I did some research. It transpired that lint collected from the dryer is an excellent fire starter if soaked in oil! And many kitchens contain a jar where waste cooking oil from deep-fried dishes is deposited. If the lint is soaked in a little of this oil, it is a very good fire starter. Unfortunately, my family are not as enthusiastic about all this as I am, which usually means I get to light the fires in winter. But, on the upside, all this shows how two waste products can become useful items.

There are myriad ways that we can all live a little better and more sustainably. The constant in this is awareness, and thinking about the choices you make at every turn. First, there is the need-or-want question: *do I just want something, or do I need it*? Then consider the quality and life span of, and ethics behind, any given product. We all know that a garment or household item being very cheap means that the manufacturing process is not ethical, on a labour or materials front. I feel great joy that I have been using the same set of saucepans for over thirty years, that the coat I wear outside will last a lifetime, and that my work pants are made from the most environmentally sound fabric possible. As more and more of us think like this, we will be giving our planet a lifeline.

Recipes for things to give away

Aside from homemade gifts like felted balls and potholders, one of the most precious things that you can give your friends and family is your time. A beautiful way of expressing this is to make them something delicious. I tend to make baked goods and confectionery, but perhaps this is because I have a sweet tooth. Here are a few of my favourite things to make, and wrap up or pop in jars for people.

Bill Granger's raspberry slice

Many, many years ago, I had the pleasure of chef and restaurateur Bill Granger coming to visit the restaurant in Kyneton to film a segment for one of his television shows. We went and foraged elderflowers and made cordial, and he made his eponymous raspberry and almond slice using my raspberry jam. The slice has become an absolute favourite of mine, but I will often use different sorts of berry jam in it, especially batches of strawberry or blackberry jam that haven't set properly because the fruit was too ripe. It's a great way to utilise sloppy jam.

210 g unsalted butter, softened

165 g caster sugar

2 tsp vanilla extract

200 g flaked almonds

2 tbsp milk

225 g plain flour

40 g cornflour

160 g raspberry jam

Preheat the oven to 180 °C and lightly grease a 24 × 20 cm tin and line with baking paper.

To make the almond topping, put 60 g of the butter, 55 g of the sugar, 1 tsp of the vanilla extract, almonds and milk in a saucepan. Cook over a very low heat until the butter has melted, then turn off the heat and leave to cool.

To make the base, beat together the remaining butter, sugar and vanilla extract until it's pale and creamy. Sift the flour and cornflour together, and add to the butter/sugar mixture in 2 separate batches, beating on low speed in between until it's just mixed.

Press the dough into the baking tin and bake for 12 minutes, or until lightly golden. Remove from the oven and leave to cool for 10 minutes. Carefully spread the jam over the pastry base, then spread the cooled almond topping over the jam. Return to the oven and bake for a further 25 minutes or until golden brown.

Mum's almond crescents

When we were growing up, we rarely had store-bought biscuits. Mum had a collection of recipes for things that she made batches of that were always in tins in the pantry: almond crescents; pink meringues; orange Viennese fingers, dipped in chocolate; and shortbread, to name a few. The almond crescents were a family favourite and are excellent to trot out as a Christmas gift as well.

1 cup unsalted butter
¾ cup caster sugar
1 cup almond meal
2¼–2½ cups plain flour
vanilla
icing sugar

Preheat the oven to 180 °C.

Cream the butter and sugar. Add the almond meal, flour and vanilla.

Roll into crescents, bake for about 10 minutes or until golden brown. When hot, toss in the icing sugar; when cold, toss them again.

Eccles cakes

The recipe for Eccles cakes is yet another that showcases my love of the humble currant. This one is an adaption of the one used by the wonderful Fergus Henderson from St. JOHN in London. If you have friends who love a good cheddar, a piece of cheese with a bag of Eccles cakes is an excellent gift.

For the filling
50 g unsalted butter
110 g dark brown sugar

220 g currants
1 tsp ground allspice
1 tsp ground nutmeg

For the pastry
500 g excellent butter puff-pastry roll

For the glaze
3 egg whites, beaten with a fork
shallow bowl of caster sugar

To make the filling, melt the butter and sugar together, then add them to the dry ingredients, mix well, and leave to cool before using.

Unroll the puff pastry on a floured work surface and cut circles about 9 cm in diameter. Spoon a blob of your cake mix into the centre of the disc and pull up the sides of the pastry to cover the filling. Seal it with your fingers, then turn it over and slash the top three times (to signify the Holy Trinity). Paint the top with the egg white, then dip it in the sugar. They are now ready to bake for 15–20 minutes in a hot to medium oven; keep an eye on them, so they don't burn. They can be eaten hot or cold.

Comfort food

Chicken soup is often given to people when they are feeling poorly; this version may be a little rich for those who aren't feeling the best, but is like a warm, nostalgic hug.

I like first to poach a whole chicken, and then thicken the poaching stock to make the soup. I don't tend to use all the poached chicken in the soup garnish, so I keep it for sandwiches or Asian-style salads.

To poach a chicken

Rinse a no. 16 chicken under cold running water and let it drain for about 5 minutes.

While that's happening, chop a peeled onion, a couple of peeled carrots and 2 or 3 celery stalks into 2-cm cubes.

Place the chicken in a large pot. Cover with cold water and then bring to the boil. Skim it. Add the chopped onion, carrots and celery, along with 1 tbsp of whole peppercorns, a clove or 2 of garlic (peeled and crushed), a bay leaf and some fresh herbs.

Add 1 tbsp of salt, and bring it to the boil. Then lower to a simmer, cover with a tight-fitting lid and cook for about an hour.

Check to make sure the chicken is cooked through. Turn off the heat, remove the chicken and transfer to a large bowl to cool for about 20 minutes. And save the broth!

When the chicken is cool enough to handle, pull off all the meat, using a fork for the trickier bits. Refrigerate.

Cream of chicken soup

75 g butter
75 g plain flour
2 L chicken stock, reserved from poaching the chicken
salt and pepper, to taste
2 leeks, sliced, washed and cooked in an extra 75 g butter

Place a heavy-based pot over a medium heat and bring the temperature of the pot up a little.

Melt the butter and then add the plain flour.

Stir constantly and cook under medium-low heat until the flour starts to turn brown and smell nutty.

Add in the broth a little at a time, similar to making a roux, while stirring constantly. Keep adding the broth and stirring to prevent any lumps.

When you've added all the broth, turn up the heat, still stirring to prevent burning, and bring it to the boil. If it is too thick, add a little more water or broth to thin it.

Turn off the heat and remove from the stove.

Season with salt to taste.

To serve, I heat up the shredded chicken with the cooked leek, pile in the middle of a soup bowl and pour the soup around it. It can be garnished with fried-bread croutes.

A plate of love

This next dish is a gift for friends that you truly care for. Taking it when you are invited for, say, an afternoon drink shows your love and appreciation.

Broad bean season is a mixed bag. There is the joy of growing wonderful broad beans, especially as you are warmed by the knowledge that, simply by growing the plants, you are enriching your soil with nitrogen and improving it for all the plants that come after it, but there is also the relentless picking, podding and peeling of your crop. When you are a little sick of doing all that for you and yours, change your focus to the positive and think of the gift you will take to friends; the thought of a new audience will give you the verve to pod another 300 grams' worth.

This dip, to me, is sheer luxury. You can make a chunky version, as per the instructions, or blend it till smooth if that is what you prefer. And the flatbreads are a delightful gift all on their own.

Broad bean dip and flatbread

300 g broad beans (podded weight)
2 cloves new season garlic, crushed
juice of ½ lemon
60 ml extra virgin olive oil
salt and pepper

Place the broad beans in boiling water for 3–5 minutes. Drain, and refresh in a bowl of iced water. Peel, roughly chop and flatten into a rough paste with the back of a large knife. Place in a bowl with the garlic, lemon juice, oil, salt and pepper, lightly crush with a spoon and mix well to combine.

For the flatbread
500 g white bread flour
10 g fine sea salt
10 g dried yeast
350 g warm water (weigh it on scales – don't just use a
    measuring jug)

Measure the flour and salt into a big mixing bowl.

Measure the water out, add the yeast to the flour and salt, and let it sit for a couple of minutes. Pour in the water and, either with your fingers, a big spoon/spatula or a bread scraper, mix the lot together into a big, shaggy mass.

Tip the lot onto a board or bench, and work the dough as follows: put your hands underneath it; lift it; slap it down on the board with a nice satisfying thwack; stretch the top of the dough out in front of you, then fold it back – taking care to do it gently, thus trapping air in between the layers. Do this over and over again – if you keep lifting, slapping, stretching, folding, and trapping air, the dough will start to form a homogenous, smooth mass without the addition of any extra flour. Once you have a relatively smooth dough, place it on the board and form it into a ball by folding the edges into the centre, pressing down with your thumb, rotating the dough, folding and pressing until you have a neatish ball.

Rest the dough by putting it back in the mixing bowl, covering it with a tea towel, then leaving it somewhere warm and draught-free for about an hour until doubled in size.

Start heating your grill plate, or light your barbecue. After the dough has doubled in size, knock it back with your fist and turn it out onto the bench. Divide the dough into tennis ball–sized portions. Once you have established that your grill plate is hot, roll the dough out as if you were making a pizza base, sprinkle with a little olive oil and place on the grill. Turn when it is nicely marked on the underside; remove when marked on both sides and cooked through – it only takes a couple of minutes. Place on a rack. Repeat the process until all the dough is cooked. If you don't have a ribbed grill, this can be done in a heavy-based frying pan.

Wellbeing

THE MODERN WORLD leaves me a little perplexed. I am not particularly good at being 'on' for as many hours a day as seems to be expected in the 21st century. Perhaps what I feel is fatigue, as I have spent much of my adult working life doing multiple shifts across the day. I have had a long battle with my mental health and, as I have found the means and the maturity to take positive steps to improve it, I am acutely aware of those who don't have this privilege. However, we are now living in a world where the discussion of mental health is becoming more and more mainstream, and the stigma I felt when not always coping earlier in my life has lessened.

That said, I do fear that the inexorable rise of the smart device that allows people to contact you at all hours of the day and night, across multiple platforms, is having a significant impact on our welfare. The barrage that can come from social media sites, email, telephone, messaging and third-party review sites leaves me weakened and, at times, nauseated. I think constantly about how to manage this in a way that doesn't have a negative impact on my business but accounts for my right to have private time.

In this age of hyper-digital activity, there are many steps I have implemented to help mitigate its effects on me. I have found that, as I have a slightly addictive nature, the compulsion to check my phone is very strong. I may check emails, or social media, for no real reason other than it's a sort of nervous tic. So, my rule for myself is – well, it's not strictly enforced, as there are days I know I need to keep a check on things – I don't always have a device on me. By not taking my phone out into the yard, I have a much more connected experience with the job at hand. I had a habit of listening to podcasts or classical music while doing boring tasks out in the garden, but I have started to eschew even this, instead taking in the sounds around me and revelling in the quiet. The absence of the phone, and its associated digital capacities, creates an environment that is not distracted and multilayered. I can concentrate, and for long periods of time, on the task I am attending to. If it is one such as basic weeding, which requires little thought, it allows my mind to work through issues or questions that need quiet thinking space. This has taken a little training, as I have found in recent years that my ability to concentrate on one thing has diminished as my capacity to operate multiple devices, flitting from thought process to thought process, has become enhanced. It leaves me feeling my mind is working in a way where it has become jack of all trades, master of none, making me feel anxious and overwhelmed.

I am very aware of the frustration it causes others that I am not connected all the time. If I don't answer a text message or an email almost immediately, the people who sent them often get quite testy, which is inevitably bad for them, as I am at peace with my choice to step away and not always be at the beck and call of my pinging devices.

I have also realised that sending a text message has replaced some basic incidental exercise. While a walk to hunt someone down is often longer than it would be in a suburban environment, it can be a lovely chance to get a bit of fresh air. If Susan has made a pot of tea, or wishes to discuss something, she now needs to come and find me. It's not always a perfect system, but the release of this tether to the rest of the world has given me welcome time, space and rest from the frenetic pace that our lives are now lived at.

As mentioned earlier, another huge step I have taken in protecting my mental health is embracing the notion of choice, understanding that no one forces me to do all the things that I do. All the decisions that I make are mine to take responsibility for. In the past, I might have blamed outside influences if I felt that I was working too hard; now I have a strong sense of what is enough or too much, and if I choose to do too much, I must accept all that comes with that. As an employer, a partner, a step-parent, a member of a community, there is always the opportunity to show, not tell. Leading by example, and being a communicative person, allows others to observe my way of finding balance and assess whether there is anything in it that could make their own life more comfortable.

All this striving for, and reflection on, a better balance so I can sustain myself to achieve all I want to do in all the spheres of my life is one reason that I have come back to observing the eight-hour day. The hospitality industry is infamous for its mistreatment of workers and its long and unsociable hours. It has become very important to me not to expect any of my employees to work more than an eight-hour day. This should hardly need explaining but, in any case, it is clear that it allows people to make their own choices and arrange their lives to suit their needs and wants. It means that if they wish to take on a second job, they can; if they wish to go home and garden, they can; if they wish to go home and sit in front of the telly for the evening, they can. From experience, I know that it is often difficult to tell your boss that you are working above your capacity and/or outside your designated work hours, and I am equally aware of the effects of too much work on the body, the mind and those around you.

This also ties in with how we manage the restaurant-related devices. As we run a very small team at du Fermier, we tend not to answer the telephone during lunch service. This is so that we can completely devote ourselves to the customers in the room. It also means that we can return messages in an unhurried manner later in the day, making sure that the customer at the end of the phone is now the absolute focus. Answering emails is done in a similar manner. We have a manual system that we like to think offers a personal-service touch, but I am sure that some of our patrons would love us to answer messages and emails twenty-four hours a day. I can't expect the people who work with me to take on this responsibility and deal with customers at all hours of the day and night, given that I won't myself. The division between work, leisure and sleep has become very blurred. I, for one, do not think that this is a positive. In embracing a more sustainable approach to life, how we operate at a personal level, with our own resources, is at the core of our existence. Sustainability is not just about using the earth's resources more responsibly; it is about better using your own.

Sleep is, without doubt, a very important part of my day. Making the decision a few years ago to stop operating the restaurant in the evening has been absolutely revelatory for my personal wellbeing. I have never been a night person; I am happiest tucked up in bed and ready to go to sleep when it's dark. The hours that I sleep change seasonally: I often sleep more in winter and less in summer – a little like the animals in the yard. The geese, the goats and the chickens all run to a clock that is not based on hours but on daylight. It seems to be a pattern that I am following more and more as I spend a greater amount of time caring for them and working outside in the garden. It is as if their needs and mine are becoming very similar.

The surprising (or maybe not) result now if I don't get enough sleep, or even rest, is not pretty. Tired, irascible, perfunctory Annie is no fun for anybody, especially me. This is screamingly obvious when the side effects of not enough rest and sleep include weight gain and systems failure in various bits of my body. As the pace of this modern world keeps getting busier, it is up to each and every one of us to decide how much to commit to the external forces at play, how much we engage with them, where our priorities are, and to try to find a place for ourselves that fits with our personal, financial and relationship values.

After thirty years of living in the country, I am trying not to become a stranger to the needs of city and suburban folk. I imagine that smaller-scale gardening, long walks and various forms of exercise replace the chores of farm life. And I imagine that reading, theatre and dining out are much higher on the agenda than they are for me, which exposes the nature of balance. For each of us, no matter where we live, our location enables us to find the day-to-day rhythm that suits us best in that environment.

When I start to analyse the choices that I have made, I question what sort of load I am willing to put upon myself. I have a full-time job at the restaurant, yet choose to do more. I garden extensively, keep many animals, write. It is no wonder that I am always ready for bed by nightfall; while I'm often tired from my day, mainly it is a wonderful, fulfilled tired. I sometimes look at my life and think how different it would be if we hadn't bought cows, goats and looked after someone else's sheep. If Susan had left it at the mouldy old trio of geese that I had and not bought more, if I had set up a poly tunnel and just two blocks of garden to grow in. Would I be less busy, would I be less tired? I don't think so, as I suspect that I would have found a million other things to do. The combination of work and leisure that I have found makes me feel profoundly happy and fulfilled, giving me hope that I may be able to keep to it for the long term.

Whether you live in the country or the city, the basic principles of wellbeing can be applied. I like to be busy; others find equilibrium by being less busy. There should never be an instance of judging another; it is a matter of personal truth. My life at Babbington Park, and quest to live more sustainably, nurtures connection, activity, learning, giving and being present. There is never a day that I don't engage with, and benefit from, all of these principles. And I am much happier

for the change in how I live and how I am, but it is deeper than just getting out and feeding the animals and watering the garden. It is also about sharing what I have with my family. To have taken two teenage girls from the city to a rural existence, and watched them grow and change. To have forged a life with a forever partner, and understood and accepted compromise. To have relocated an elderly parent into a family environment, rather than a nursing home. We have taken many of the resources we have and shared them in a manner that is kind rather than exploitative, and it is this kindness and sharing that is the backbone of our life here.

And there is also all the laughter. So many mistakes, so many silly times to share and greet with a raucous laugh.

Recipes to nurture yourself and others

Food is an essential part of our wellbeing – it is the fuel that keeps us going. As a restaurant cook, I have had long periods of eating poorly, as, for many years, I did not have regular mealtimes. The net effect of this has been that I have struggled with my weight, as I have a genetic predisposition to be on the heavier side of the ledger. Weight gain has never sat well with me; it is too much pressure on my knees and feet, and too much pressure on my state of mind.

Our industry has also struggled with the knowledge that sometimes the food served to customers is not the healthiest option for them. Sharing good food and the enjoyment of food is integral to our happiness, and our sense of participating in family, friendships and communities. It is joyful for most people to sit down to a celebratory feast, to indulge in excesses and to delight in others' company. We cannot eat like that every day, though.

Added to this, given our very busy lives, both the affluent and the less well-off frequently make poor food choices, eating too much of the wrong things at the wrong time. It is one of the reasons that eating plans such as the 5:2 diet, where you spend two days eating very little, have such popularity. They are also a wonderful educational tool to alert us that we actually eat far too much and can easily survive on less. For the less affluent, the problems are different, as the further down the socioeconomic ladder we are, the more attractive cheap, highly processed food that, of course, has very high salt and sugar contents can be. Cooking nutritious cheap meals at home is less widespread than it was thirty years ago. However, with educational programs in schools about food and cooking, and public conversations about nutrition, obesity and food provenance, I have hope that this trend may one day be reversed. I believe that those who can afford to make better choices about their food should, as it strengthens both the market for and the ideology around eating better, and opens up options for those who struggle to afford to make healthier choices. Financially supporting sustainable agriculture helps make those farms more viable and allows prices to come down, so that less wealthy people can afford more nutritious options.

I even find some comfort in the rise in popularity of the electric slow cooker. While I have never been fond of those plastic electrical cooking appliances, I understand that not everyone has the same working knowledge that I have of stewing and braising, and that putting an inexpensive cut of meat and some vegetables in one of these appliances is a far healthier and cheaper option than buying a pre-made meal packaged in plastic.

In my work kitchen, I have tried to institute a regimen where the staff gets to eat a quick meal before the customers start arriving at noon for lunch. This is known colloquially as our 'diet lunch'. I try to make us a delicious meal that is low in fat, has little or no carbohydrate component, is delicious, quick to prepare, easy to eat, and will stop us from grazing or picking our way through the next four hours of service. They are often dishes that are thrown together from the items in my pantry and almost always have no connection to the food that I cook in the restaurant.

Kingfish sashimi salad

This is not an everyday diet lunch for us; it is a very special luxury. When I get a fish delivery to the restaurant, sometimes I spoil us and order a side of line-caught kingfish, my favourite fish to use raw. This dish is very ad hoc in its quantities and seasonings, and is all about a personal-taste approach.

SERVES 8
1 side kingfish, about 800 g
4 small cucumbers
2 green apples
handful snow peas
pickled ginger
soy sauce
apple cider vinegar
wasabi powder, mixed to a paste

Skin and clean the kingfish, removing any red flesh lines, then cut the fillet in half lengthways. Cut nice regular sashimi-style pieces about 4 mm thick, and set aside.

To make the salad, julienne the cucumbers, apples and snow peas and place together in a bowl. Throw in a little shredded pickled ginger, a slosh of soy and a slosh of apple cider vinegar. Toss, and check the seasoning to see if it needs correcting.

Arrange the slices of fish down the centre of each plate, smear with wasabi paste, and place an artful handful of the salad on each line of fish.

Chermoula chicken and cucumber salad

Chermoula is one of my favourite North African spice blends, and it works particularly well in our simple lunch dishes. It adds a great deal of flavour to something like a chicken fillet that is a little bland. It is made from a blend of cumin, coriander, garlic, onion, chilli, lemon and a little paprika.

SERVES 2
1 small skinless chicken fillet
1 tbsp chermoula
large handful salad greens
1 small cucumber
apple cider vinegar
2 tbsp natural yoghurt

Rub the chicken fillet with the chermoula and a pinch of salt.

Warm a non-stick pan to medium heat and place the chicken fillet in the pan; cook it slowly and gently, so the flesh doesn't dry out, turning once. This should take about 10 minutes. When just cooked, remove from the pan and allow to rest. Place the leaves in a bowl, chop the cucumber into small chunks, and add to the lettuce. Dress with apple cider vinegar. Slice the chicken very thinly, toss through the salad, and serve with a dollop of yoghurt on top.

Chicken and wombok soup

This is a soup that I make often, as I frequently have chicken stock on hand, and/or leftover poached chicken or meat that has been stripped from roast chicken carcasses. It can also be made by stir-frying a chicken thigh, and then building a stock and flavour base from the stir-fry pan. Instructions for both are below. And, of course, if you are hankering for some carbohydrates, this is a perfect dish to which to add a handful of either wheat or rice noodles.

SERVES 4

1 tbsp sesame oil

½ small chilli, chopped

1 tsp grated fresh ginger

1 garlic clove, crushed

8 wombok leaves, chopped into a chiffonade

1 L chicken stock or water

1 cup shredded cooked chicken or 2 chicken thighs

soy sauce

3 spring onions, thinly sliced

Warm the sesame oil in a pan or a wok; add the chopped chilli, ginger and garlic. Cook gently to release the flavours, turn the heat up and add the wombok. Toss until it is wilted, add the stock, bring to the boil, add the chicken, and bring back to the boil. Season with soy sauce and spring onions, and serve.

The from-scratch version

Shred the raw chicken thighs and toss in a little soy sauce, and set aside.

Warm the sesame oil in a pan or a wok, add the chopped chilli, garlic and ginger. Cook gently to release the flavours, turn the heat up and add the shredded chicken. Cook over a high heat until the chicken is cooked through, and add ¼ cup stock or water to 'deglaze' the pan or wok. Reduce that liquid to almost nothing, and add the wombok. Toss until it is wilted, add the stock, bring to the boil, add the chicken and bring back to the boil. Season with soy sauce and spring onions, and serve.

Simple summer fish salad

This is a dish that I love to make for us in late summer, with all the best sun-ripened produce from the garden: tomatoes, basil, a little sweet pepper and cucumber. It is dressed with a bit of good olive oil and a squeeze of lemon juice. Fish is something that we recognise as a luxury; we in the restaurant are passionate about using sustainably caught fish and only having very small portions that are bulked out with lots of vegetables.

SERVES 4

4 small flathead fillets
2 large ripe tomatoes or 300 g small ripe cherry tomatoes
1 small red or yellow pepper
½ garlic clove, crushed with salt
virgin olive oil
salt
2 small cucumbers, chopped in small cubes
4 sprigs basil, stripped and chopped
4 sprigs continental parsley, stripped and chopped
large handful rocket leaves
1 lemon

Remove any bones from the flathead fillets; set aside. Chop the large tomatoes into small wedges or cut the cherry tomatoes in half, and place in a bowl. Cut the pepper into fine strips and add to the tomatoes. Add the garlic, a slosh of olive oil and a good sprinkle of salt. Toss and allow to macerate for ½ hour or so. Heat a non-stick or lightly oiled pan to a high heat. Add the flathead fillets flesh side down; turn onto the skin side to finish cooking. Place each fillet on a plate. Add the cucumber, herbs and rocket to the tomatoes. Toss. Place handfuls of the salad over the fish. Drizzle with a little oil and a squeeze of lemon juice.

Adieu and good luck

I look forward to many years here at Babbington Park and cooking in my little restaurant, du Fermier; to watching my wild, chaotic flower gardens grow, in delightful contrast to the disciplined rows of vegetables and pruned fruit bearers. I have a slight tendency to want to hurry life along a bit, so that I often will plants to leap and grow before their time, but I must silence that urge. I know that waiting is part of the joy of creating a garden and that all corners of our world here will be more glorious year by year.

The path that I have chosen over the past dozen years does not make me an expert in sustainable living; I am just a regular person trying to step a little more gently on the earth and to live a kinder life. Yet, I feel that there are more and more like me, who want to make a change for the better: to simplify their lives, to lessen their footprint, to have time for the things that matter, for each other, to reconnect with skills and lessons that have been forgotten for a while. Whether it is seen as naivety or not, I believe that if we all do something, no matter how small, it will make a difference.

When I look into the young and eager faces of our girls, I see the promise and hope of a generation that is acutely aware of their, and our, responsibilities to the planet and to the climate. If for no other reason, I want to live better for them, so they get to enjoy this earth and realise their dreams as I have.

Acknowledgements

To Susan and the girls, thank you for always being patient with me, especially when I bring home more animals.

The team at du Fermier, both those who work with me and our wonderful customers, thank you for all your support.

Thanks to Kieran and James, who get their hands dirty with me and laugh at my stupid jokes.

Great thanks to the team at Thames & Hudson Australia, especially Sally Heath. Sally, thank you for your guidance, candour and encouragement, as you untangled my scribblings and made them what they are now.

Index

with meat 205–6, 210–11,
250–1
with medlars 143
with nuts 138, 141–2, 148
with parsnips 135
with pears 144–6
with pomegranates 147
with potatoes 136–7
with pumpkins 121–3
with quinces 148
with radishes 128–9
with shallots 133–4
with stone fruit 140, 143–4,
147
with swedes 129
with turnips 129
see also recipes
corn 93, 121
Cornwall, UK 41–2, 155
recipes inspired by European
settlers 45–51
cows 160, 203–4
crabapples 74
crafts *see* arts, crafts and DIY
cress family 81–2, 123–4, 127
see also broccoli; brussels
sprouts; cabbage; cauliflower;
kohlrabi; radishes; swedes;
turnips
cucumbers 81, 84, 93, 118–19
currants 64, 92, 103–4

darning 250
Daylesford, Victoria 3–4
deforestation 40–1, 45, 158
digital activity 79, 263–4

DIY projects *see* arts, crafts and
DIY
Dja Dja Wurrung people 39
Djab Wurrung people 58
dogs 206–8
do-it-yourself projects *see* arts,
crafts and DIY
domestic animals 206–9
dried fruit *see* prunes
du Fermier, Trentham
beginnings 10, 15–18
customer service 265–6
diet lunch 269–70
employee rights 265–6
menus 17–19
opening hours and meals
offered 19–20
purchase of building 19
recipes 21–34
ducks 76, 164, 205

eggplants 81, 119–21

fabrics *see* textiles
farming 6–8, 41–3
see also animals; gardening
fatigue *see* wellbeing
Fearnley-Whittingstall, Hugh 6–7
felting 249–50
figs 142
flowers
in Babbington Park gardens
67, 232–4
floral recipes 234–41
food sovereignty 6, 15, 20
see also farming

Recipe index